Instant
Content Marketing
Success

10 Tips from Top Content Marketing Experts

Bob Tripathi

@bobtripathi

Hashtag: #IET

Join the conversation on Twitter by following the
#Hashtag #IET

Praise for the book

This is the most complete and comprehensive playbook on content marketing that is out there. It offers a perfect balance between the fundamental knowledge needed to conceptualizer content marketing strategies and a practical toolkit full of ready to implement ideas. Bob does a phenomenal job laying out the core infrastructure needed to build and scale content marketing efforts including ideal process layouts, org charts and resources. It is a must read for both young marketers and seasoned executives who are looking to build robust content marketing campaigns.
- Ashish Rangnekar
Co-Founder, BenchPrep

Bob is an open and honest individual, with an extremely bright mindset. He truly understands content marketing. Instant Content Marketing Success is a book that outlines all the appropriate avenues one needs to succeed in the content marketing space. With informative outlines and examples throughout, Bob helps those that are both new and experienced in social media, search engine optimization, and lead generation to gain valuable insight into new and proven ideas that work. This is definitely a book that all business owners need to own.
- Dr. Steven Lee,
EVP and Co-Founder at Opternative, Inc.

Bob Tripathi is a proven expert in digital marketing. I've personally watched him spread this knowledge to many fellow entrepreneurs in helping accelerate their companies' early stage growth. I'm excited to see this wealth of knowledge gathered into one book.
- Mike Shannon, Co-Founder, Packback

As a lifelong B2B marketer, I have always believed that content is king, but I would argue that it has never been a more critical component of the marketing mix than it is today. Everyone is a publisher, and in this book, you'll find actionable insights to help launch a content marketing effort, or take yours to the next level. From building a buyer persona and researching keywords to link building, social media and beyond, you'll gain practical advice from the very practitioners who are redefining content marketing today. Whether you are a professional marketer, business owner or independent consultant, this primer will put you on the path to content marketing success.

- Sima Dahl, MBA
America's Personal Branding & Social Networking Champion
The Sway Factory, Inc. | SimaDahl.com

This is the most effective book I have read on content marketing. A step-by-step instructional guide without any marketing jargon. We are a growing startup and have been looking for an internal process to create content and use inbound marketing. This book makes for a straightforward read and it helped our entire team to understand the process of content generation. A must read for every startup!

- Piyush Kedia
Founder & CEO, SymbiosisHealth

Finally. A easy to digest, content marketing How-To. Tripathi has a special way of breaking down complex concepts into bite size tangible pieces that are ready-to-use. I've already implemented several concepts in to my marketing initiatives.

- Ethan Linkner
Co-Founder, VLinksMedia

DEDICATION

This book is dedicated to all lifelong learners in quest of knowledge. Heartfelt gratitude to all educators who spend a big part of their life in spreading knowledge. Finally, to all Instant E-Training cohorts who motivate us everyday to create quality education content and make our professional life so fulfilling.

The only thing that interferes with my learning is my education
- Albert Einstein

CONTENTS

INTRODUCTION

Over the years I have had the good fortune of working in small, medium and large businesses that have had one thing in common which is to produce content to acquire customers. Around 6-7 years back, companies wanted to create content to please the Google gods, if you will, and in turn rank higher in Search Engine Results Pages (SERP's). This created a rush where companies of all sizes across the board wanted to churn out content daily which I have come to call the mad content creation race. Today that has changed from producing content for search engines to producing content for users to generate leads and sales. This has been a healthy shift as the quality of content that companies produce has gone up since companies have the end user in mind. So let's step back a bit and ask ourselves why do we need content marketing?

Well, content marketing is a key marketing tactic that enables us to ensure that the shelf life of content that we produce is longer and to repurpose old content that we may not have produced for the original purpose of marketing.

What is content marketing?

Content marketing delivers high quality information, void of any promotion. As marketers we are all aware of the noise and clutter we have to fight through on a daily basis. It is easy to get shouted down, but content marketing offers something of use to our target audience and as such breaks through the chaos to attract attention. Content marketing allows us to educate and entertain our target audience. Your brand, spokesperson, product or company as a result is positioned in the right place. Prospects, customers and the public are engaged and both decision makers and customers can be influenced. Quite a few perks from one area of marketing, right?

Why do you need it?

Content marketing is trusted by customers. Unlike other promotional campaigns that can become both tiresome and interruptive, content marketing is well received by customers. There are very few brands and companies and in fact even products that have not embraced social media as a tool. Content marketing is in the same ecosystem as social media and actually feeds it. Your message is delivered in multiple ways and through a variety of platforms and as such your customers begin to believe your message. Although content marketing is not free, it is relatively cheaper than other campaigns and boasts a longer shelf life.

How is this book organized?

We think the best way to learn about a new topic like content marketing is to hear view points from multiple experts. So I have brought together some leading content marketers, that also happen to be trainers at Instant E-Training, all of whom bring great thought leadership on the topic of content marketing but also have deep "in-the-trenches" experience. Each chapter has contribution from a Subject Matter Expert on a specific topic like Arnie Kuenn on Keyword Research, Heidi Cohen on Content Strategy, and so on. I have organized this book in a linear learning manner ensuring that we progress through each chapter just like you would if you were to start a content marketing campaign.

I hope this pocket sized book serves as a handy guide for all things content marketing. We at Instant E-Training hope you enjoy!

CHAPTER 1

TEN STEPS TO BUILDING A CONTENT MARKETING STRATEGY

WITH HEIDI COHEN

Introduction:

In marketing, strategy plays a crucial role as it sets the blueprint on how successful your program is going to be. The flow of marketing is about planning, strategizing, execution and measuring results. No where this is more truer than in content marketing. In order for your content marketing to succeed you need to get planning and strategy in place. Deciding on a strategy before setting out to execute is a key factor in determining whether or not you will be successful in your content marketing attempts. In this chapter, we will start with content marketing strategy with none other than Heidi Cohen. Heidi is an industry respected expert who has been practicing what she preaches from a long time and so it made perfect sense to have her start with our first chapter on 10 steps to building a content marketing strategy.

But before we dive deep into strategy let's look at the exponential growth of content marketing with the help of this chart.

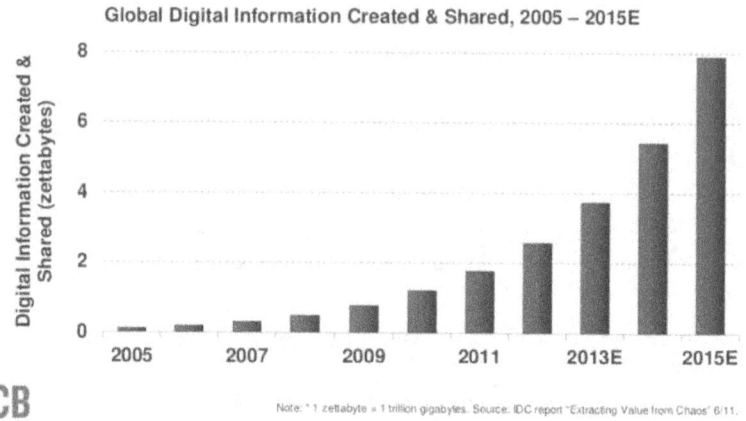

According to a IDC's Extracting Value from Chaos report, it is seen that there will be 8 Zeta bytes (yes, zeta bytes) of digital information created by 2015. This growth has been exponential starting from 2009 and with the widespread adoption of social media this trend has skyrocketed as seen in the chart above.

Why you need Content Marketing?

There are many businesses who still question as to why they need content marketing to grow their sales. Here are five reasons why businesses should embrace content marketing:

1. Is trusted by customers

When you write a blog post or publish an eBook, chances are those pieces of content will be trusted more by your customers than say the marketing copy on your homepage or on your product pages.

2. Supports purchase process

In this age of continuous connectivity, there is no linear marketing funnel as we know it. A sound content marketing strategy can help guide your customers down the marketing funnel to the final conversion.

3. Feeds social media

With the widespread adoption of social media, content essentially is what drives this whole sharing, retweeting behavior. It's not just the cats and dogs pictures that people like and share on Facebook but also content that your target audience likes. Your content distribution is relatively easy as good content feeds your social media channels.

4. Delivers your message multiple times so customers believe it

The biggest advantage of content is you can produce the same content in different types of formats so your customers can consume it on a variety of formats like blog, eBooks, infographics, video and so on. And when you deliver your message multiple times in multiple types of formats then chances are your customer would believe it.

5. Is relatively less expensive (though *NOT* free!)

Even though the content you produce internally is sort of free it is not entirely free as there is a cost of time spent on producing that piece or pieces of content. That cost comes from the time you spent researching, writing, editing, designing that piece of content.

So now that we have established why content is important and why we need content marketing let's jump right into creating your content marketing strategy. Let's get started with our 10 Steps to building a content marketing strategy:

1. Establish your content marketing goals:

When developing your content marketing strategy, be clear on what you are trying to achieve. Goals may vary per campaign or industry for example: are you trying to build your brand or generate leads and sales? Knowing what you are trying to do before implementing a content marketing strategy, will get you on track for success.

2. Know your target audience:

If we are trying to market to everyone, we are reaching no one. Identifying and being conscious of who we are trying to reach is a must when exploring content marketing. Start with a simple demographic and then expand. Think about their lifestyle, what they are interested in, who influences them, their past purchases and their personal goals. Filling in the blanks may take some time, but creating as full a picture as possible of who you are marketing to will lead to a better campaign and most likely, better results.

3. Determine information needs:

What information are your customers looking for? Providing something they need and want makes you a useful source. This helps you to build trust as a resource and encourage brand engagement. If you are not sure what your audience wants from you, do some user testing. They may want answers, product information or how to tips. Make sure any ratings or reviews you provide are accurate and legitimate. You will want to source these from an impartial third party with no affiliation to your brand. Honesty is a must in these situations! The possibilities are endless and there will be a huge amount of variation depending on what product or service you are providing.

4. Select Content Formats:

Once you have established the kind of information your following wants, you must decide how you would like to share it. Informative content can come in many forms so you must decide what works best for your brand and your clientele needs. For some, text based information may work whilst others may better consume video. Certain situations require audio or an infographic. They summarize a huge amount of easily received content. EBooks are also a great way to share tips and tricks with your following. Once you have started to relate to your audience and have developed a better understanding of your demographic, you will be in a better position to cater for their needs. If you go down one track and determine an alternative route would have been a better choice, don't worry you can always change your tactics!

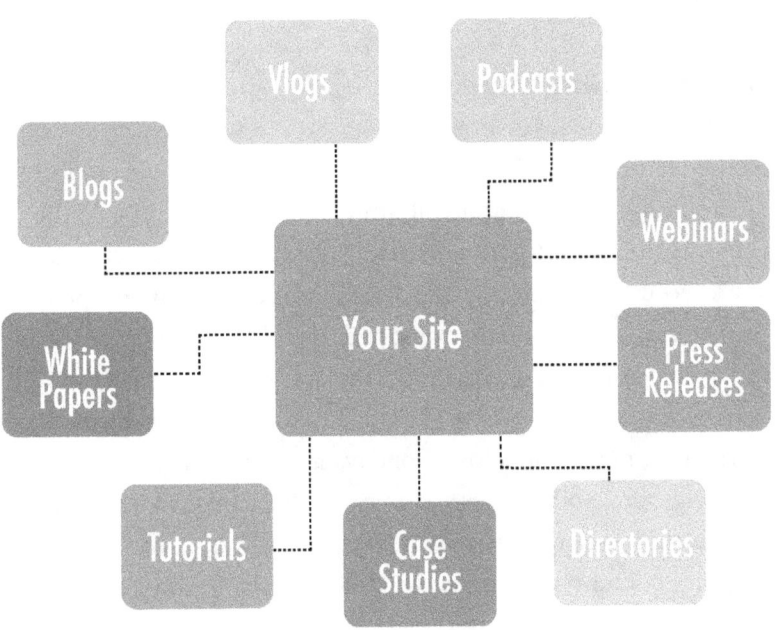

5. Tell your stories:

You can share your tales but you must also allow your audience to do the same and keep in mind it is not always about you. Share something funny that happened to your team that day. For example, if everyone arrived in unintentionally wearing the same color. This will both humanize your brand and allow you to encourage engagement from your following too, you never know what story they have that can relate to your plight!

6. Brand your content:

Your content needs to be recognizable from miles away if you are trying to attract traffic through building your brand. You have to take everything you do and make it consistent. Colors, text, sound, and audio even the structure of your language. Do you want your people to be easily recognizable through consistent clothes? If so you will have to consider your visual representation. If you think of a store that has uniformed staff for example, you will always associate them with the brand.

7. Develop an editorial calendar:

An editorial calendar ensures you stay on track with your content marketing efforts. You know in advance what kind of direction your posts should be going in and will ultimately save you time in the long run. To create an editorial calendar, you must decide what kind of structure your calendar will take. Think about how many posts you will be sending out on a daily basis and what kind of metrics you wish to track. Factor in seasonality and holidays as these will allow you to embrace a variety of content such as seasonal tips on how to cook the perfect dinner. People love holidays and enjoy talking about them so this will give you an opportunity to humanize your brand and directly relate to your audience. Assessing marketing promotions and developing content categories will allow you to be prepared and effectively take advantage of key times to share your news and utilize marketing efforts. Your calendar will also mean that you can establish recurring content features and decide on your major content offerings. Another huge benefit of an editorial calendar means that you can do some keyword research and enhance your content's SEO in advance.

	Sun	Mon	Tues	Weds	Thurs	Fri	Sat
Week 1							
Week 2							
Week 3							
Week 4							

Source: © 2013 Heidi Cohen http://HeidiCohen.com

8. Optimize search and consumption:

If no one can find your content, no-one can consume it. It is very easy to get too close to your brand or business and as such become removed from what it is that your audience is actually searching for. You must start by finding out! Your headline is just as crucial as your content, so you will want to ensure that it is attention grabbing. Make your content more visually appealing with some eye-catching images, as a huge amount of text can be repelling. Craft your content around one keyword phrase. Doing some research on frequently searched keywords that are affiliated with your service or product will help you to determine what your audience is in fact searching for.

9. Distribute and promote content:

Once you have successfully created your content, what should you do? Effectively distributing and promoting content will play a huge role in determining how successful your content marketing efforts will be. Start by placing it on your owned media, then promote and direct people to it from your social media platforms. Include links in all communications and incorporate your content into offline interactions. It is important to insure that people are aware of and can find your content, otherwise all your hard work won't bring the rewards they should. You will also want to leverage your physical presence. Position yourself in front of the people that are likely to need your content. Attend events relevant to the topics you have covered in your content and spread the word!

10. Track results:

You have established your goals, implemented a strategy and worked on creating and promoting your content. Now, you must track the results that you have received thus far. What were you trying to accomplish? If you were trying to increase traffic, did people come? Have you generated leads? It is time to assess how successful you have been in reaching your goals. To make things really measurable, you need to create a sense of urgency by including a promotional code, a call to action or insert a tracking into any links that you share beforehand to measure the response.

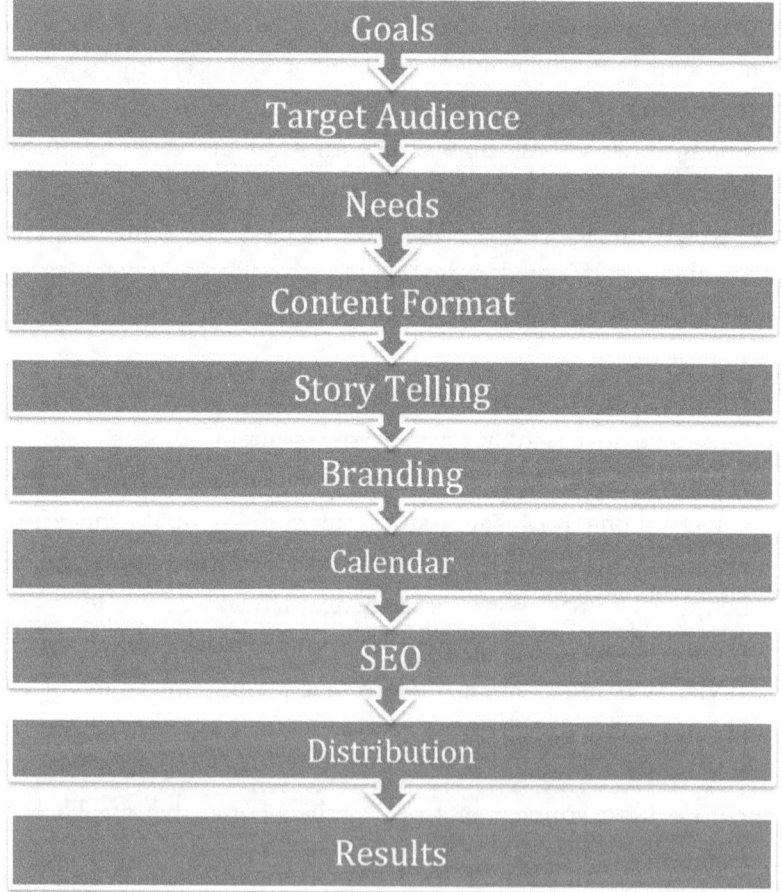

Summary:

As you can see content marketing is about establishing goals for your target audience and then determining their needs. Content marketing is also about selecting the content format that your customers can consume along with keeping your branding and other needs in mind. Finally, it is all about being focused with the help of a content calendar and then optimizing your content and distribution and measuring results. Again, content marketing is hard but then if it was easy then everyone would be doing it!

CHAPTER 2

IDENTIFYING AND DEVELOPING THE BUYER PERSONA

WITH SHADE WILSON

Introduction:

In the last chapter we looked at how critical it is to start with a content marketing strategy. After you have your initial strategy in place, the next step I recommend is creating your buyer persona. Personas started gaining popularity mainly after Alan Cooper's bestseller "The Inmates are running the asylum" published in 1998. In the book, Alan Cooper introduced the use of personas as a practical interaction design tool. Since then the use of personas has transcended into other areas as well with marketing being one of them. Over the past few years I have experienced first hand the benefits of using personas into our marketing with content marketing being one of the biggest beneficiaries of using personas. Since we all are in this race of creating immense amount of content, it is imperative that we create content with not a one-size-fits-all approach but more creatively by using personas. In this chapter, I am pleased to have Shade Wilson whose company Scalability Project has done some extensive work in the area of persona creation talk about the topic of developing your buyer persona. In the next few pages, you will read not just about the importance of buyer persona but how to go about developing your ideal buyer persona. Over to Shade Wilson now.

You have to understand your audience so that you can market to them accordingly. Developing buyer personas allows us to do just that. Instead of marketing our product, tool or service, we are answering the question how can we help solve the problems of our buyer. A buyer persona is a simple representation of your ideal customer.

To get started with buyer persona, you should develop and understand a collective of your customer segments.

- Demographics
- Behavior
- Motivations
- Challenges & Pain Points
- Concerns

Your targeted customer segments are important as what matters to one audience segment might not be important to some other audience segment. We all have marketing challenges to overcome, be it our customer or brand. The truth is the challenges are larger than we credit them and can create adverse ripples. Pains may vary throughout an organization but it is a key part of a content marketing strategy is to incorporate all these challenges.

Example: A the Chain Reaction:

If there is an issue with a product or service, a ripple effect of disruption is created. The reliant party may need help from a business or a supplier so as not to lose time. This will shift up to the managerial level as they are unable to meet user demand which leads to internal frustration and discomfort. The Vice President of operations will be made aware that there is an inability to hit goals as employees cannot reach targets without a solution. The CEO, will be informed who will have to have a missed target meeting and so on, until the entire ecosystem has been affected. Your content needs to address all these aspects. You need to think how your content can address all the challenges of people at different stages of the organization.

Building a Persona:

We need to talk to our customers, we might think we know them but building a buyer persona should provide us with better insight. Segment your customers, keeping in mind you are not just looking for one fix as an important on as we are now aware that there are

ORGANIZATION ROLE:

What is their role in the organization?

If I ever found a "your service" who

I'd recommend them to everyone I know.

Scalability Project

many pains in one ecosystem. You will need to dive into the trenches and talk to people on the frontline; your sales team and customer service. Hearing directly what issues they are being informed of and the feedback they receive will be incredibly beneficial. Building a buyer persona does not rely on only one phase, you must gather information from different angles to ensure the validity of your end result.

Persona Interview breakdown:

When interviewing a customer you want to get certain information out of them. Maintaining consistency ensures the relevance of your results. Start with their role, where they fit in the process and what are their needs and challenges. Ask them to identify a pain point, for example: What are the issues they are facing and challenges they are trying to overcome? Zoom in on their response. Understanding problems is a huge part of knowing where your brand or product can help. Inquire about a power point: Who else in the organization is involved and what is their level of control? This will help you get to the decision makers.

Why do we ask questions and what to ask?

In order to develop your buyer persona, you will need to come up with a set of power questions that you can utilize. Here are some of the sample power questions you can ask:

- Tell me your role and what else are you responsible for?
- Can you tell me about the process you go through to…?
- Who else is involved? How many levels and challenges should my content be addressing?

Remember to keep your questions open-ended as it allow you to extract so much more information. You want people to talk during these interviews as this will provide you with a huge amount of insight. When you keep your questions open-ended, your subjects will provide you with much information.

Vision Questions:

Following open ended questions, the next set of questions you need to come up with are what is called Vision questions. Vision questions help you probe your customers more into their long-term vision for your products or services. Few vision questions you should include:

- How they see your service helping their organization
- How does it impact the organization
- What part of the service is most important?

Pain Questions:

The nest set of questions you should come up with when developing your buyer persona is to ask them about their pain points. Few pain questions you should include:

- What type of service do you find yourself needing help fixing?
- Are there certain challenges you always have to overcome with these services? This will bring great background information about what needs to happen and how to proceed.
- Magic wand question: Ideal scenario about what would work better.

Value Questions:

What matters? What do you value most in service? Let them tell you what is important. This is very important for content marketing! Understanding what people care about leads to a more accurate content marketing effort on your part. Focusing on what you think they care about is a waste of resources.

> **Your secret weapon question:** Complete the sentence: If I ever found a service that _____ I would recommend it to everyone I know.

Tip: As part of your research efforts, you could consider creating a buyer persona template. Keep it simple to understand what they are trying to solve, their pains and where to go from there.

Humanizing research entices you to empathize with problems and to envision a solution. Being upfront will help you find a solution! Keep in mind what they are looking for and how you could fit in to benefit the customer. Understanding goals is a key component of accomplishment both with buyers and from the buyers perspective. Remember, you have to focus on multiple pains, not just on one level.

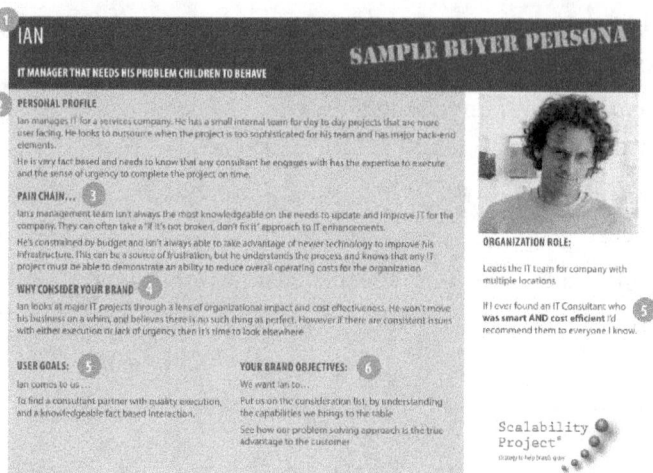

Summary:

As you can tell the process of developing your buyer persona can be laborious and time consuming but the benefits of getting them done can be multifold. One being you have a clear idea on what target customer you should develop your content for. The other could be the type of content your target customer is most likely to consume. Lastly, developing your customer persona enables you to operate your content marketing program in a more strategic manner where you are aligning your content marketing with the goal of driving conversions for your business. Finally, I leave you with this quote by Shade Wilson on personas. Enjoy!

GREAT MARKETING IS NEVER ABOUT YOUR COMPANY, IT'S ABOUT THE PROBLEMS YOU HELP YOUR BUYER SOLVE.

CHAPTER 3

KEYWORD RESEARCH FOR CONTENT MARKETING

WITH ARNIE KUENN

Introduction:

Keywords are the cornerstone of content marketing. Keywords have intent and when keyword research is done in a strategic manner it can provide intelligence to drive your content creation efforts. Keyword research is also not something that you want to do just once and then forget about it but the best content is created when there is a continuous process of researching keywords then creating content and then again refining it based on actual keywords that your customers use to find you. In short, keyword research should be a continuous process and not something that you want to set it and forget it.

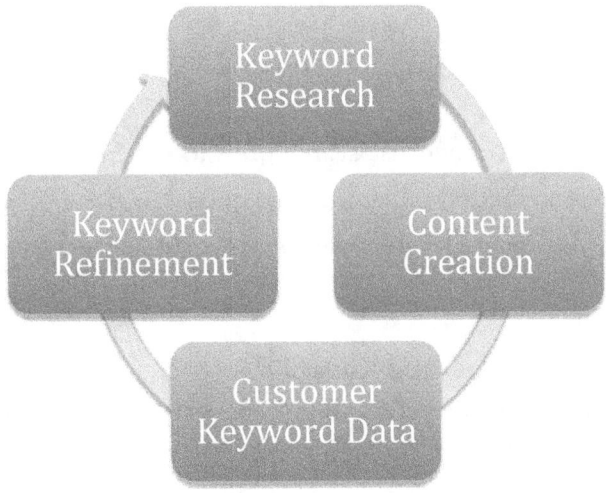

In this chapter we will read all about keyword research from Instant E-Training's trainer Arnie Kuenn and the best ways to approach keyword research for content marketing. Over to Arnie Kuenn now.

Keyword Research for Content Marketing

With content marketing you are striving to provide relevant, valuable content to your customers without selling or interrupting them. Instead of pitching your product, you are delivering information that makes your potential consumer more informed before they make a purchase. The beauty of content marketing is that if you deliver, you become a loyal source to your customers and thus they will ultimately reward you with their business. Relationships are now created first with information, not with people.

Marketers should not approach content marketing as a way of driving a quick ROI (Return on Investment). Content marketing does not provide a quick 30 day ROI per se but long-term payoffs can be huge! Studies show that both B2B and B2C companies with 101 to 200 pages generate 2.5 times more leads than those with 50 or fewer pages. Similarly, companies that blog 15 or more times per month get

5 times more traffic than companies that do not blog. A recent study by GroupM found the following buyer statistics:

- 93% of all consumers use search prior to making a purchase.
- 86% of searchers conduct branded queries.
- 90% of buyers click on organic links versus sponsored ads.

Inspire me, Educate me, and Answer me

A recent About.com study found that users searching online exhibit three distinct human behavior patterns that can be grouped into three distinct categories of Inspire Me, Educate Me and Answer Me.

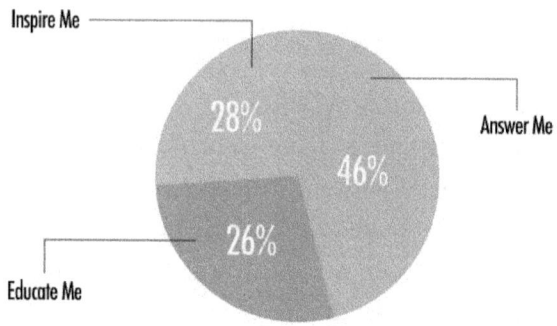

Inspire Me:

28% of all searches fall into this category of content. This means marketers should develop content that inspires creativity and offers endless choices to searchers. These users are often open minded and want to be led so they consume content in multiple formats.

Educate Me:

26% of all searches fall into this category of Educate Me type of content. As a result, marketers should create messaging that is informative and provides a way for users to learn more about topics from multiple angles, aligning content that provides in-depth information and resources.

Answer Me:

46% of all searches fall into the Answer me category. This tells us that 46% of all searches want exactly what they ask for delivered in a way that allows them to get it as directly as possible. Marketers should feature product benefits front and center and align content in a way the presents quick, easy-to-find answers.

The Long Tail of Keywords

Even though marketers have been using this technique of keywords long before the term gained popularity in Chris Anderson's bestseller book "The Long Tail: Why the Future of Business is Selling Less of More."

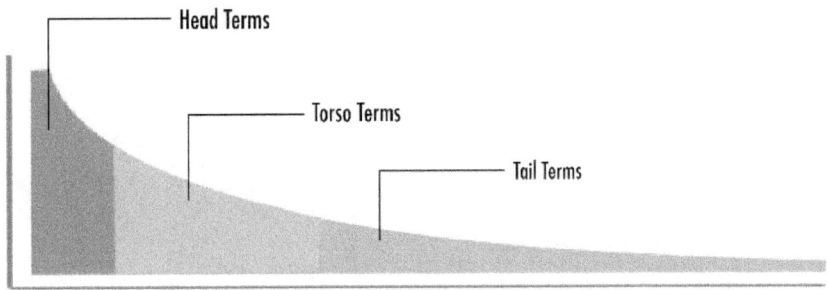

As you can see in the chart above a one or two word keywords are known as head terms and typically they have massive keyword search volume. Which means lot of people are using one or two word query on search engines. That also means that the competition to rank higher for those keywords is also intense (if not impossible). This is where the beauty of long tail keywords comes into play. A long tail keyword, considered to be three words or more, is where the competition is not that intense and chances are your content has more probability to rank higher up on search engines. So your long-tail keyword research becomes the key! When a long tail keyword is searched, the majority of people will click on the first search result. If you are ranked lower down, you will be overlooked. People are extremely quick to refine their search when they have entered one or two keywords and see the enormous amount of data that they have received. We all pause and start to think more about what we specifically require. A study by Optify further drives home that point where they found that long tail keywords get higher click thru rate than many of the top head terms.

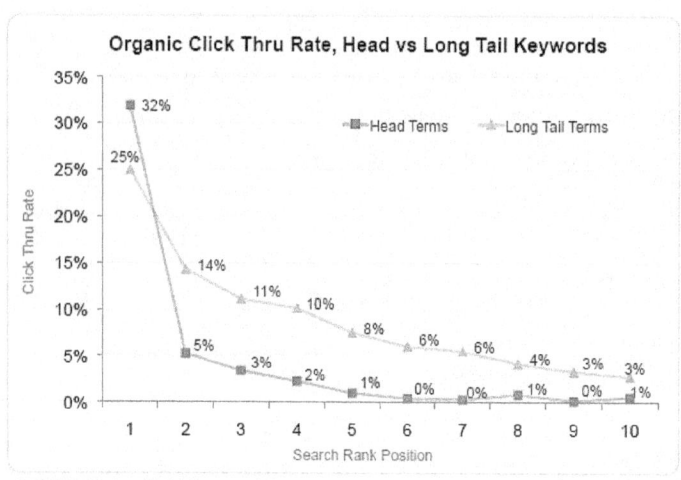

Start with Internal Keyword Research:

As often as overlooked it is but your customers could be a great source and a great starting point when you start with keyword research. Gather the employees that interact with your prospects and your customers. Ask them what questions they get asked repeatedly by your customers either through email, phone, live chat or any other forms of interaction you use with your customers. This is the foundation for your content and will help you to provide something of use.

Keyword Research tools:

There are literally hundreds of keyword tools out there that you can use for keyword research but start with a free tool like Google AdWords or Soovle and begin your formal keyword research with some of the recurring keywords that you have gathered thus far and see what suggestions you receive. Soovle is a great suggest as you type site that can help with some quick keyword research. It gathers search as you type keyword suggestions from multiple sources including major search engines and Wikipedia and Answers.com. This can be a quick way to do some keyword research on the fly!

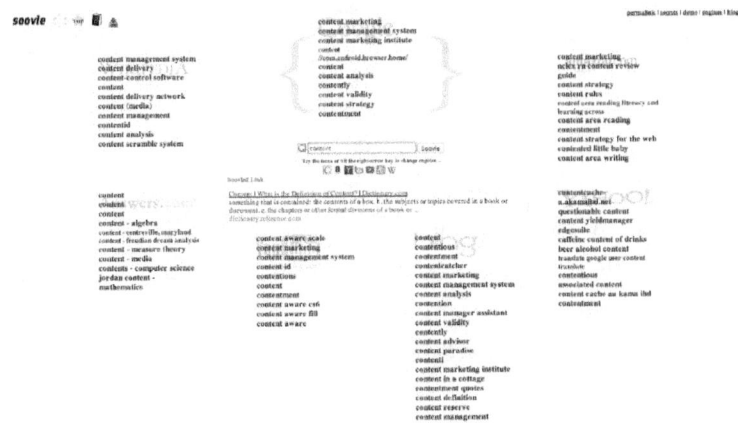

Use Google: If Google is suggesting a phrase it means that a whole load of people are looking for it. Your business can create content to ask the questions and try and win those search results. YouTube is another great way to embrace free market keyword research. Take note of all the suggestions that you receive.

Searches related to **visit the grand canyon**

fly to visit the grand canyon   visit the grand canyon **in november**

best time to visit the grand canyon   visit the grand canyon **in december**

best way to visit the grand canyon   visit the grand canyon **from las vegas**

visit the grand canyon **from phoenix**   **best place** visit the grand canyon

Google Discussion & Blog search:

Where people are discussing industry relevant topics. Spend some time reading their questions and identifying their concerns. This will make sure you stay in the right area.

A good source is Google's discussion tab as seen from the screenshot below:

Should I **go to the Grand Canyon**? - Yahoo! Answers
answers.yahoo.com › ... › United States › Other - United States
No answers - 17 hours ago
I'm planning a trip to USA in November. I am mainl...

Is visiting the Grand Canyon really worth it? - 8 answers - Jun 5, 2011
Can you visit the Grand Canyon's North Rim in April? - 3 answers - Feb 3, 2011
Visit to Grand Canyon during November end ... - 4 answers - Oct 31, 2009
Where do you fly in to visit the Grand Canyon? - 3 answers - Jul 30, 2007
More results from answers.yahoo.com »

Visiting the Grand Canyon? - M/SO Community Forum
forum.maplewoodonline.com/.../visiting-the-grand-canyon/p1
27 posts - 18 authors - Jan 3
Hubby and & I will be in Las Vegas for a meeting, the second week of March. Would
like to tack on a visit to the Grand Canyon, as I have never ...

Las Vegas to **Grand Canyon** and Back | United States Forum ...
www.fodors.com › Forums › United States
12 posts - 11 authors - Jun 11, 2012
If we do Grand Canyon, are there must stop places along the way? About us: Only
going to Vegas to see a particular show. Otherwise, we are ...

Visiting Yosemite & **Grand Canyon** | United States Forum | Fodor's ...
www.fodors.com › Forums › United States
44 posts - 10 authors - Mar 10, 2012
My wife and I - we hail from Malaysia - are now planning for our trips to the Yosemite
& the Grand Canyon, after visiting Boston. We are thinking ...

Grand canyon march trip | United States Forum | Fodor's Travel Talk ...
www.fodors.com › Forums › United States
7 posts - 5 authors - Jan 9

When you have acquired all your keywords, create a spreadsheet. When you have a clearer idea of what direction you could take all these keywords in, you should create an editorial calendar to see what times you could best leverage this content. You will need to factor in holidays, events, product launches etc. When you have laid your general concepts, you take the best ideas you have generated from your keyword research and start to think when would be best for use to utilize that content. How will you market, where will the content go, what will the title be and where will you get your images or video from? Share through social media channels but try not to get too hung up on social shares, sometimes even the highest ranking pages haven't been shared. .Identify your opportunities when you have completed all your research. Fill any voids that you identify and keep in mind that when you see a gap in the search market that it is for the taking. If you don't get your content in there, someone else will!

	Title	Content Type	Keywords
277			
278	How to Write a Newsworthy Press Release	Blog Post	how to press release
279	What is a Press Release?	Blog Post	press news release
280	Press Release Distribution: Where does your news go?	Infographic	release distribution
281	Best Press Release Examples by News Category	Blog Post	press release example
282	50 Ways to Promote Your Press Release for Free	Blog Post	press release for free
283	Exploring the components of a Sample Press Release	Blog Post	sample of a press release
284	Top 10 Outreach Techniques for Influencing Press Contacts	Blog Post	press contacts
285	PR Newswire vs PR Web: How they Compare	Blog Post	pr newswire
286	Does Your Online PR Make the Grade?	Blog Post	online pr
287	How-To Guide for Press Releases	Free Guide	press releases how to
288	Free Press Release Tools & Tips	Blog Post	free press release
289	The Right Occassions to Issue a News Release	Blog Post	news releases
290	Press Release Template: Disecting an Effective News Release	Infographic	a press release template
291	How to Format a Press Release	Blog Post	press release format
292	Top 40 List of the Best Press Release Sites	Blog Post	press release site
293	Using PR to Promote Your Next Conference	Free Guide	conference press release
294	Why Your Business Should be Doing Press Releases	Blog Post	business news release
295	5 Key Components for Creating an Online News Release	video	online news release
296	What is a Social Media News Release	video	social media news release
297	Criteria for Evaluating News Release Services	Blog Post	news release service
298	The Best Free News Release Distribution Channels	Blog Post	free news release distribution
299	Digital News Release vs Standard Press Release	Blog Post	digital news release

Summary:

As mentioned earlier in my chapter introduction, keyword research is not a one time thing where you set it and forget it. Instead keyword research should be a continuous process where you refine your keyword list regularly. The tips that Arnie shared in this chapter are golden and should serve as a great starting point with your keyword research. So I will reiterate what I stated in the opening line of this chapter – Keywords are the cornerstone of content marketing so make sure you have created a solid process so that you do not miss any opportunities when it comes to content creation.

CHAPTER 4

CONTENT MARKETING FOR SEO

WITH BOB TRIPATHI

Introduction:

We looked at how to approach keyword research for new content marketing ideas in our last chapter with Arnie Kuenn and in this chapter we look at optimizing your content for search engines. Search Engine Optimization or SEO is basically a practice that we follow where we use certain best practices like tagging, copy optimization and other elements of a website to make it perform optimally on search engines. This also includes building relationship with other sites where they link to your site. This is exactly where content marketing comes into play - once you have truly optimized content that can be found on search engines then chances are other sites will link to your content and thereby increasing the number of sites that link to you. But before we go any further lets start by looking at SEO timeline and where we are after almost 20 years of SEO as we know it.

SEO Timeline – Post Google Era

SEO or Search Engine Optimization has matured as a marketing tactic right from the early days of SEO which is around 1995. I know some of us SEO's nostalgically remember those days when ranking higher up on search engines was relatively easy. Throw in some keywords, optimize title tags, build some links and that's about it. Well, let's face it – those days are long gone. In today's new world of SEO or Google 4.0 we need more than keywords and links. We need social signals, we need good usability and so on but most importantly we need content. Google, with about 70% market share (depending on who you listen to) has undergone massive algorithm changes over the years. Here is a brief timeline on the SEO changes:

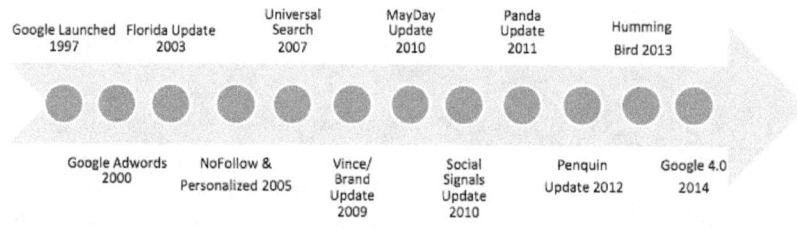

As you can see from the timeline above, Google tweaks its algorithm every year or so to keep itself relevant and most importantly to keep the spammers from exploiting its algorithm. As a result, businesses need to constantly keep up-to-date with changes so that they do not lose the traffic coming from search engines.

The 2C's of SEO:

To simplify Search Engine Optimization is all about, as I like to call it the 2C's – Content and Credibility. You can also refer to it as On-Site

SEO and Off-Site SEO:

In the chart above, On-Site SEO is the optimization that happens on your site or servers and off-site SEO is essentially activities you do through other sites to boost your site SEO. Content is about the content on your site and credibility is about other sites linking in to your site otherwise also known as incoming links to your site.

This can further be broken down with the graphic below:

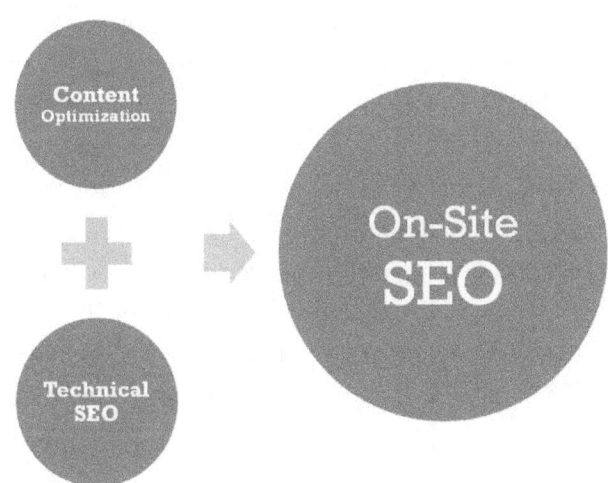

On-Site SEO is about content optimization and your server level settings. Server level settings include how you set up your site redirects, folder structures, TLD's and more. We will come back at Content optimization little bit later in this chapter. Now, let's look at

Off-Site SEO:

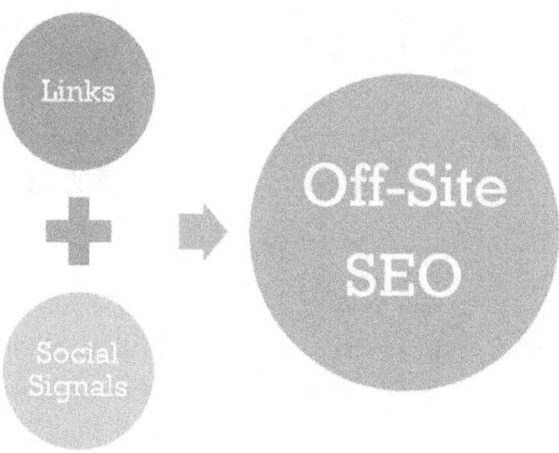

As you can tell from the chart above, Off-site SEO is about links pointing to your site and the social media signals. Now, link building in the Google 4.0 world is a lot about relevancy and authority of sites that point to your site. In short, focus on quality of links and not the quantity of links that point to you. A case in point, many VC funded companies get good amount of buzz in the marketplace but they may not all be relevant to their business as they are not from industry relevant sites. So if you are a food delivery company and you get all your links from education companies then that is not very relevant and not in your industry link profile. The other component of off-site SEO is Social Signals. Social Signals is about how the social media love that your company gets whether be it through Facebook shares, Retweets, LinkedIn Shares and most important of all the +1's on Google+.

Content Optimization for SEO

Since this book is about content marketing, it is important that we focus on the core elements of Content optimization for SEO. Here is a graphic that explains that:

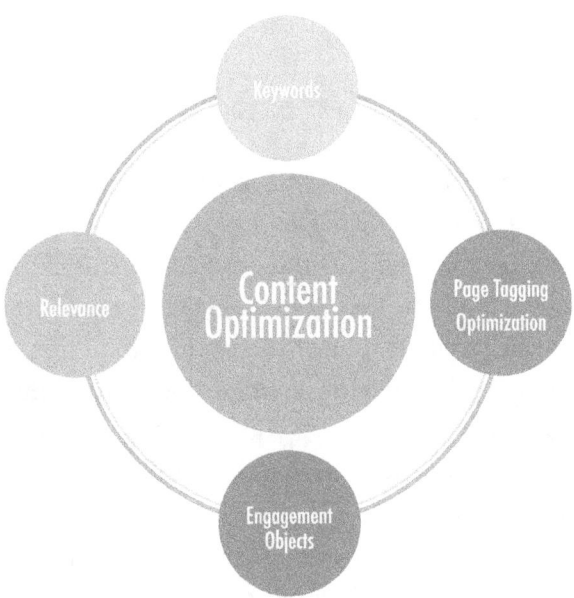

As the graphic above explains, content optimization can be broken down into four main parts namely:

1. Keywords
2. Contextual relevance
3. Engagement objects
4. Page Tagging/Optimization

Keywords:

Keywords are the cornerstone of Search Engine Optimization. Keywords basically are the intent of your visitors and prospective customers. Strategically researching keywords and then using it on your page is what optimization is all about in a nutshell. There are tens of books written on the subject and hours and hours of training videos on Instant E-Training so it would out of scope for me to go in-depth here. To put it simply – keywords have intent, keywords have meaning and importantly keywords is how you drive inbound traffic from search engines to your site.

Contextual Relevance:

The content that you produce on your site should be relevant and on-topic. In other words, businesses need to create content that is relevant to their business and to their target audience. Importantly, you want to create content that is on-topic and focused on a single topic. The best optimization to me is no optimization that means that if your content were focused on a single topic then the keywords would flow naturally. So let's say you have an e-commerce store where you sell watches from different branded companies, then create content pieces that talk about each brand name and why the watches from Brand X is superior in quality and so on. This way you create content pieces that are focused on a single topic and chances are your keywords are already built-in to the topic itself. Plus, you are relevant to your target audience since they are watch buyers looking for watches.

Engagement Objects:

Engagement as a term can mean many different things to different people depending on what side of aisle you are in. For SEO, a page level engagement means what kinds of objects you have on your site like video, graphics, ratings, reviews and more. The more engagement objects you have on your site the better it is as it increases the total time spent on your site by your visitors. There more time a visitor spends on your site the better it is not just for your final conversion but it is also one of algorithm factors for SEO.

Social Media Monitoring for Marketing Intelligence

Video presentation by: Chase McMichael
Total Running Time: 18 Minutes
Skill Level: Intermediate
Racing 4.50 (3 Votes)

Watch Social Media Monitoring for Marketing Intelligence training video for your
$29.99

Buy this Video   OR   Become a Member &
Watch All Videos

Description:

The first step in social media for many companies is actively listening to custome But as social media is evolving, the same way listening to customers is not enoug social world you need to leverage social and marketing intelligence through socia insights by integrating social and business data. In this video session, you will hea evolving your company's social strategy - from monitoring to listening and from l

The sample screenshot from Instant E-Training's website shows how we include a preview video, has ratings, commenting feature and of course relevant page copy. These objects help in increasing the total time spent on our site by our visitors and chances are the more they interact with our page the better our final conversions get. So find out what those engagement objects are for your business and include them on your site.

Page Tagging & Optimization:

Page tagging and optimization is about how well do you include your HTML Meta tags, image optimization tags and optimize your body copy for SEO. After all there is an O in SEO and that stands for optimization. In the next section let us look at the page level elements of optimization and the importance of each one of them.

Anatomy of an optimized page for SEO

Since we covered the basics of SEO, now let's focus on one of the most critical components of SEO and that is on-page optimization. The graphic below shows a sample page from Instant E-Training video detail page.

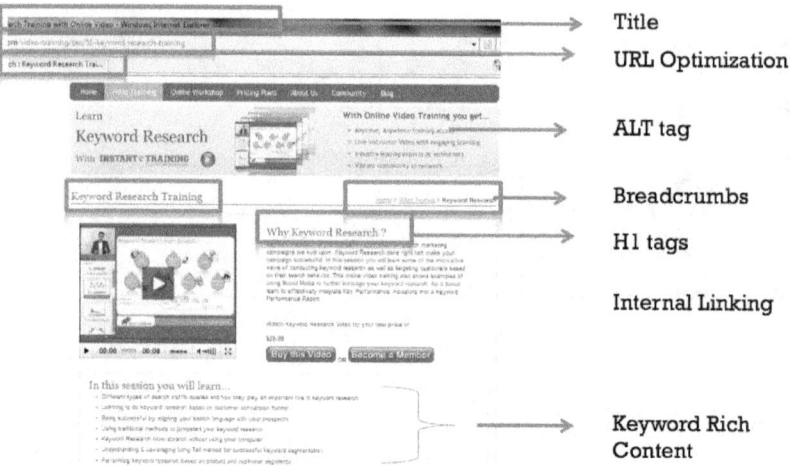

Let's go into details on all the main components of on-page SEO:

HTML Title Tag:

The title tag goes on the top of the HTML document. Each page should be unique and as a result each page should have its own unique title tag. The title tag is encapsulated between the HTML title tag like this

<title>Your unique title should go here </title>

It is a good practice to limit your title tag to be between 40-69 characters.

META Description:

This is the part that you do not see on the page but rather is seen as a snippet in search engine results pages like the example below:

Mens Shoes, Boots & Footwear | Sports Authority
www.sportsauthority.com/category/index.jsp?categoryId=3079720
At Sports Authority, we understand this, and strive to carry the greatest selection of top **men's running shoes**. From big names in men's running footwear like Nike ...

A META description should be written just like how you would write a PPC ad copy since a good description can drive up your Click Thru Rates on search results.

It is a good practice to limit your META Description tag to under 200 characters.

URL Optimization:

A simple URL structure has multiple benefits from a SEO as well as from usability point of view. A good URL that is optimized should describe what the page is about. And if the page is on-topic then chances are you would have used keywords. Here's a look at two different types of URL – one is optimized and the other is not

URL Example 1 -

http://www.instantetraining.com/video-training/social-media/social-media-strategy

 URL Optimization

In the URL example above the URL is descriptive about what the page is about. Since it accurately describes the page it also includes a keyword. The other element to note is how the URL is structured that takes into account the folder structure and if anyone simply looks at the URL they can tell that it is a page about social media strategy.

http://www.yourdomain.com/category-shoes/product-main/family.jsp?categoryId=766061&cp=3077570.3079720

On the other hand the URL above is not search engine friendly as it is missing keywords, is not descriptive of what the page is about and finally has dynamic characters like "equal to" and "ampersand" signs.

ALT tag:

Sometimes images do not load up in the browser and as a result ALTERNATE text should be used. ALT tag should be used for every image on your site including your logo.

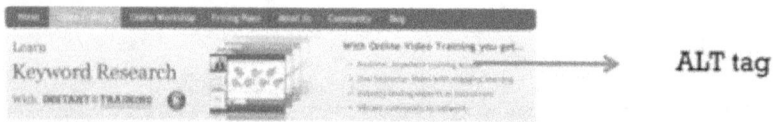

ALT tag

Breadcrumbs:

Just like the classic Hansel & Gretel story Breadcrumbs are always a great addition to any of your pages on your site. Benefits include both from SEO as well as from a usability point of view.

Breadcrumbs

H Level tags:

A useful HTML tag is H level tags where H means Heading. Usually they go from 1 to 6 with 1 being the highest. Search Engines sometimes give more weight to H1 tags as the theory is if the text is in H1 then it must be the headline and very important text. In HTML it is written as <H1>Elements of SEO</H1>

H1 tags

Internal Linking:

Internal linking is important as it allows search engines to discover pages on your site. This means that you want to strategically link to your internal pages on your site starting from your home page and then linking pages internally.

Internal Linking

Keyword rich and relevant copy:

A common myth is there has to be a minimum of 250 words on a page to make it SEO friendly. Again that is a myth long circulated on the internet. The fact is as long as you have page copy that communicates what the product or service is to the website visitor than that should do it. Use the four elements of content optimization that were recommended earlier.

Keyword Rich Content

Link Building

Link building is an critical part of SEO. After all, Google's algorithm is based on links or PageRank. Link building is a broad topic to write about and beyond our scope, I will say this – link building should be a natural outcome of your content marketing efforts. In short, if you create great content then chances are more people will share it and in turn you will build links in an organic manner.

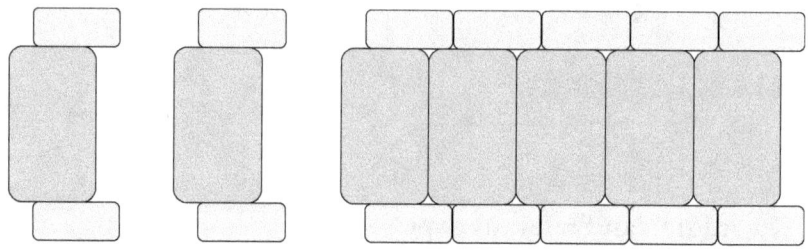

Link building can further be grouped into permanent links and temporal links. Permanent links are links that retains its value for a long time like links from directories, association sites, and more. Temporal links are short-term in nature and mainly is an effect from content shared on Twitter and other social channels.

Permanent Links	Temporal Links
• Directories • News Sites • Associations • Conferences	• Blogs • Twitter • Content Syndication

Other important elements of link building are:

- Quality of Site
- Topic and relevancy of site to your business
- Social Signals

Types of Content can be optimized:

There is a great quote from one of industry thought leaders and Instant E-Training speaker Lee Odden of TopRank marketing "What Can be Found Can be Optimized"

In other words, anything can be found on search engines can be optimized. Some examples of different content types that can be optimized are:

- **Text pages**
- **Blog**
- **Videos**
- **Images**
- **PDF's**
- **Apps**
- **Press Releases**

Summary:

In this chapter I tried to explained SEO and how it relates to content marketing. You might find more value in this chapter if you are just getting started with SEO. The thing with SEO is there are foundational elements that every business needs to leverage but the trick is sustaining it and incorporating it into a process so that you do it over and over again as long as you keep publishing content.

CHAPTER 5

CONTENT MARKETING FOR SOCIAL MEDIA

WITH BRIAN CARTER

Introduction:

Social Media has changed the way we communicate and interact with each other. Twitter and Facebook has become the Radio and Television of this generation. I can just imagine what it would be like for marketers when Television came about and how marketers tried to capitalize on it. Social Media is still in its infancy but as a marketing tactic it is here to stay. That simply means that businesses and marketers in particular need to be strategic in how they approach social media. In this chapter, we have one of our go-to-trainer for all things Social Media and Facebook Brian Carter. In this chapter, Brian will walk us through the new realities of Social Media followed by seven social media content marketing plan. You will also read about Facebook posting rules and the posting ratio you should follow. I am sure you will find all the tips golden and worth its weight in gold. Over to Brian now…

Social Media – Reactive or Proactive?

As they say the playtime on social media is over and it is time now for serious business. That means companies need to stop being reactive and be proactive with their social media program. The big question that every company need to ask is are you just reacting in social media or is your company actually moving forward toward your bigger arching marketing and sales goals. The chart below illustrates the difference between taking a reactive and a proactive approach on social media. Well, I am guessing we are honest enough to identify where we are in the social media process.

Stop Reacting. Move Forward.

Is your brand just reacting in social media or
Are you moving forward toward your marketing and sales goals?

REACTIVE	PROACTIVE
Monitor keywords	Lead conversations with your content
Consumers choose conversation space	You choose conversation space
What are people saying?	What are we influencing them to say?
Whats going on with my brand?	What does my target buyer already like and share?
Put out fires	Enhance brand perception

Social media is an excellent resource for content marketing due to its capacity to enable viral content. In this chapter, we will be considering the best way to approach structuring posts for the purpose of content marketing.

7 parts of the social media content marketing plan:

1. **Goals**- Clear, quantified social media goals, plus an understanding of how they fit into your other corporate goals.

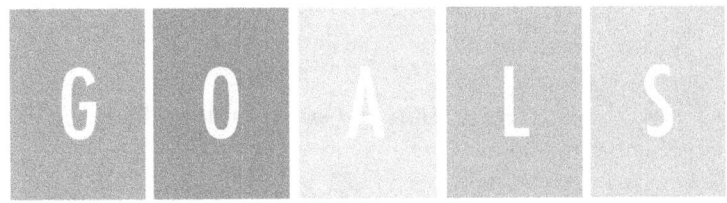

2. **Metrics**- That fit your goals and how you'll track them.

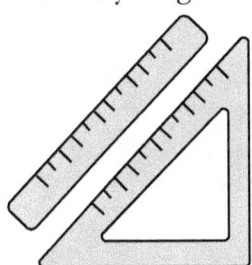

3. **Content Marketing plan**- What you create, how you curate, when and where you will promote it.

4. **Audience-** Deep understanding of the personalities of your customers. Who they are and what they like.

5. **Social advertising plan** and smart budget allocation

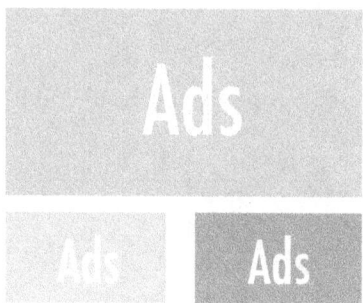

6. **Community themes-** Compelling group ideas that will attract your customers and add value to them.

7. **Shareable, Likeable Facebook posts-** Plan the content (images and text) of your next 90 Facebook posts, to last you three months.

Planning: The aforementioned seven areas are a great foundation for you to build on. We may all have different aspirations for our content marketing successes, this seven part plan is applicable to most and will help to ensure that you do not stray from your path to content marketing victory!

Remember: when a Facebook post is shared, it means followers valued it enough to want other people to see it too. Shares can be difficult to get but offer a better insight than likes about what content is resonating well with your prospects.

Defining your B2B and B2C goals is so important to ensure you place your content on the right platform. Analyzing your audience will help you determine this. Social media is largely about who people are not what they are searching for. Does your audience send an average of eight tweets per day but only updates their Facebook every month for example? If so, by focusing all your efforts on Facebook you are rarely if ever reaching the people you want to.

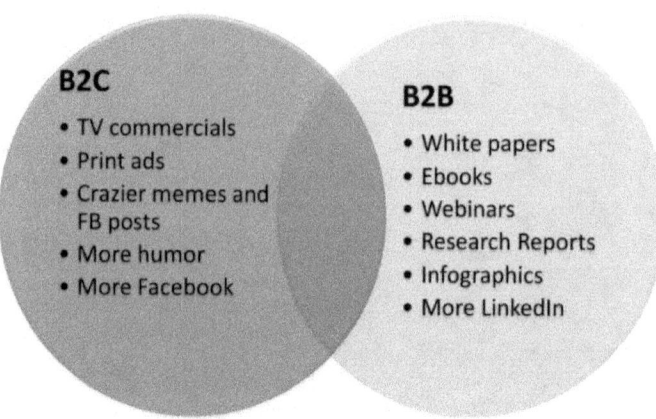

B2C
- TV commercials
- Print ads
- Crazier memes and FB posts
- More humor
- More Facebook

B2B
- White papers
- Ebooks
- Webinars
- Research Reports
- Infographics
- More LinkedIn

Consider your content marketing plan. B2B or B2C makes a difference. B2B can seem boring on social media, yet advertisements and groups are the best way to get leads on LinkedIn. Decide upon a B2B community theme and create a LinkedIn group around this topic. You can include your company name at the bottom of the page but should try to maintain a community feel, otherwise people will be deterred. Allocate an employee the job of controlling the group which in turn will help get your content shared. You can use your content as a conversation starter, but accompany it with a call to action such as a question. Ask people their opinions and they are likely to read what you have shared so that they can give an informed answer which will help drive your engagement. Track what is effective and what is not, if you see something that has been well received, try to replicate this success. When you see posts with low engagement, avoid similar content for future campaigns. Don't be afraid to use visuals to encourage engagement either, an infographic can convey the same message as a text based post but be more appealing as the content is easily consumed.

Trying to post 100% original content is unrealistic and would be a drain on your resources to attempt to generate enough. Curating content is a great way to fill your content void and also reinforces that you are not simply all about self promotion. Think about what inspires you, the posts that you see that you want to repost or the post that inspires you to create something. Curated content are the things you like to repost or inspire you to create something.

Facebook posting for B2B:

Don't get attached just to shares, keep in mind which posts are getting leads. Shares are great, but not an overly frequent occurrence. If you see a post that is doing well or in fact one that needs a little help, avail of the pay to boost option which will fuel reach more than solely relying on organic reach. Stay relevant, you can't promote

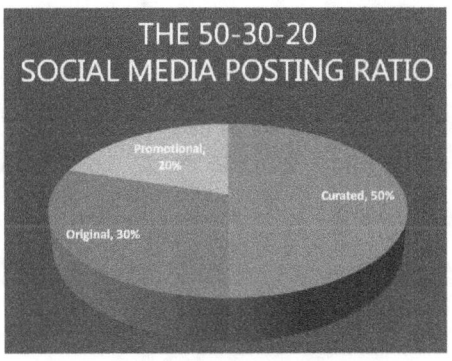

holidays that are over for example, so be sure to utilize your budget effectively.

Social media is an effective, cost efficient resource for boosting your content marketing efforts. Define your goals before you begin and do not be afraid to tweak your efforts if you are not receiving the reach you are hoping for. Get creative and have some fun!

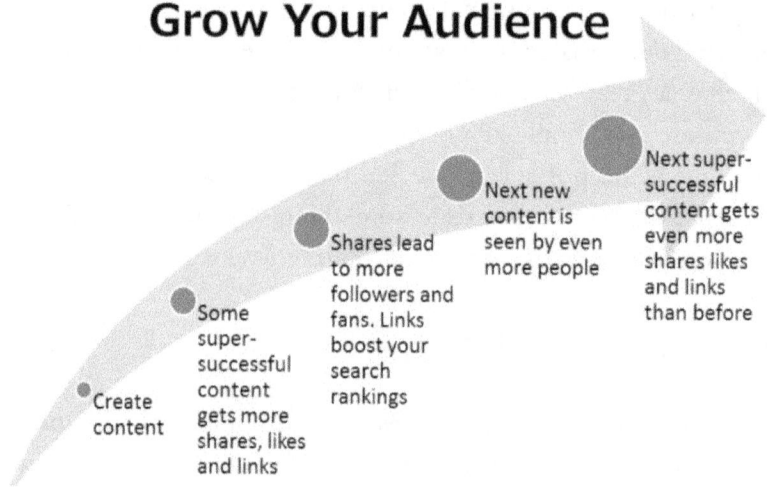

Summary:

If there is one thing I would like you to take away from this chapter then it is how to create a proactive approach on social media. Your social media, just like your business, needs to have a proactive strategy in place and Brian articulated that point well. The other key takeaway from this chapter was Brian's clearly defined parts of social media content marketing plan. My suggestion would be to take each of those point in isolation and create a strategy around it. Only then you will have a clear and well defined social media strategy for content marketing in place. Remember, you can leverage your social media channels strategically to distribute your content only if you have a well defined plan. As it goes, social media playtime is over so let's get serious as social media is here to stay.

CHAPTER 6

VISUAL CONTENT MARKETING

WITH MATT SILTALA

Introduction:

Instagram has been the fastest growing social media site in human history and surpassed other social media giants like Facebook and Twitter in terms of active usage. No wonder, Facebook snapped it up for a mere $1 billion. Moreover, as smartphones becomes cheaper and calling plans flexible, the smartphone adoption will grow further driving this adoption. The chart below by eMarketer shows US Instagram users and penetration.

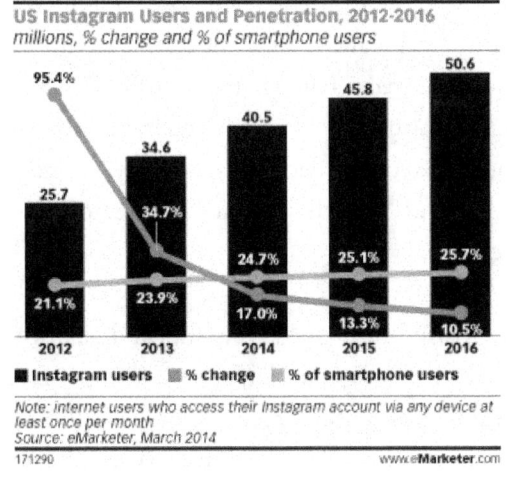

Pinterest is not far behind. Pinterest has one of the largest concentrated female base of users and according to a recent Mashable post it found that Pinterest drives more traffic to publisher sites than Twitter, LinkedIn or Reddit combined. In short, sites like Instagram and Pinterest have proven that consumers prefer visual content far more now than ever before. This has forced us to create content that is more visual in nature and hence it is called Visual Content Marketing. In this chapter, we have Matt Siltala of Avalaunch Media discuss with us the importance of Visual Content in Social Media and what specific tactics we can employ to make the most out of it. Here's Matt on Visual Content…

Visual Content in Social Media:

As a business, you have to know that it is not just important but essential to be on social media. We are very distracted these days and we don't want to be bored with reading thousands of pages of text, which is why we are leaning towards visual content. We want to be able to consume and digest content efficiently.

Michael Troiano, CMO of Actifio claims "Social media is the best way to reach your most influential customers and the only way to reach your most cynical ones." Social media has progressed significantly over the past few years. Traffic has increased, pretty much every demographic is now on one platform or another. We love it because it is a cost efficient, easy way to stay connected to people we know and brands we are interested in regardless of geographical location.

Every platform throughout social evolution has moved towards a more visual layout. The original platforms were not created for visual purposes so Pinterest arguably created a visual monster and the rest just followed. Now they have all moved in this direction and increased their user numbers substantially. This is something that we as marketers should see as a major hint about what content people are interested in. Here are some stats to further drive home that point:

- Images get 50% more interaction than other content.
- Photos get 7x more likes on Facebook and 10 times more shares.
- 80% of pins on Pinterest are repins.

Images make people react and experience an emotion. Text from a glance does not have the same impact.

Coming back to Pinterest, let's look at the ten pins of Pinterest success!

1. Uploading your own images some of the time:
This is fine, but pinning gives you the best opportunity to go viral. Meaning? If you include an image in your blog and then pin it from there, you are giving yourself a better chance to go further.

2. File names become your image titles:

Be sure you name your files accordingly. "Chocolate_cupcakes.jpg." will rank better than "April2014_20134567_009.jpg." This applies to content that matters and that you want people to find. Your personal page you may not care as much about so you can stick with the default name.

3. Remember re-pinning, liking and commenting:
All play a strong role in where your image will appear. Make sure you pin from a variety of sources instead of just one site. Do not pin form one URL. You must remember that this is social networking and you must focus on the social aspect. You are part of this community and as such you need to be proactive.

4. Include your title in the image to make it eye-grabbing:
If you are creating an infographic, eBook or a how to guide and intend to display it on Pinterest, that main big image should pop. It is what people will either be immediately drawn to or overlook, we all know how many chances we get to make a first impression so make sure you take advantage of yours. This will ensure that you stand out from all the other boards. With visual content marketing, if you are blending in you are not doing it right!

5. Settle for a short caption which includes your major keywords:
You have up to 500 characters, but a long description annoys other pinners as they feel it messes up their Pinterest grid. Make sure you edit any images you upload on Pinterest. By default, you cannot include a link so you must go back to edit it. Not making your content likable will result in a loss of traffic for you. People may think what you have shared is great, but if you are not easy to find, they won't bother.

6. Research Pinterest to see what catches your eye:

This will really help you to create your own content. If something is drawing you in during your research and it is getting a lot of likes, shares or repins use it as inspiration. Do not however just copy word for word or image for image!

7. Don't forget Pinterest is a social media, not an advertising platform:

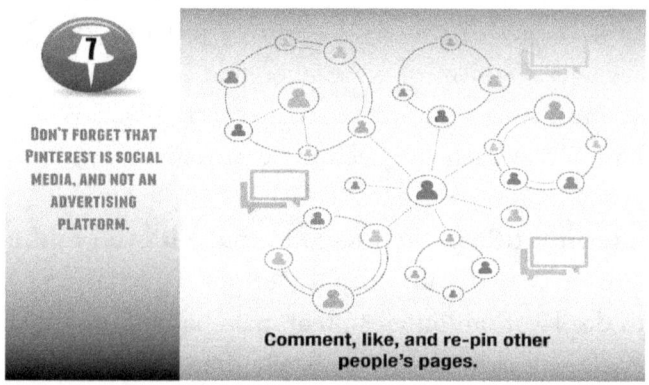

DON'T FORGET THAT PINTEREST IS SOCIAL MEDIA, AND NOT AN ADVERTISING PLATFORM.

Comment, like, and re-pin other people's pages.

Comment, like, and repin other people's pages. You are not going to succeed with Pinterest if you are not treating it for what it is. You can pin it, you can like it and leave comments. Make yourself known! If you are always engaging and sharing people will begin to do the same with you. You have to build relationships first.

8. Name your board accordingly:

Make sure your variety of boards are keyword-rich. These boards are actually ranking now so you want to ensure that you are easily found and your content will be search engine friendly.

9. Optimize your website:

Make sure people have an option to pin your product or follow you on Pinterest. The same theory is necessary for all your social media badges. The key to social media is to empower your following to do so with ease.

10. Expressing your brand and your personality:

You want to narrate and capture your unique voice and portray it through Pinterest. If you have a product or service relevant to a holiday you should structure boards around it and by using your unique voice you can strive to stand out from your competition. They may have a similar offer to you, but you may say something that resonates more with them and therefore gain the sale. Inspire people with your visuals and show them ways that they can use your product. You are more inclined to commit to trying to reenact creating an idea that you have seen with your own two eyes than you are one that you have read about. The visual element can be the sway point so optimize your content through inspiration by making it visually stimulating.

So how do businesses succeed using visuals in Social Media?

90% of information submitted to the brain is visual and images process 60,000 times faster than text, which is why Pinterest is thriving. Create a publishing calendar. If you are creating infographics, how many are going out per month? How many memes will you publish? This will help your followers know what days they can expect content from you and you will establish loyalty. Start with what is working. Use current news and stay relevant. Visual breakdowns are more effective than text versions. They are efficient, help people to stay informed and are not time consuming. Always watch your competition to see what you can learn.

Remember: Infuse personality, know your audience, name your boards smartly, have a theme, tell a story and know your audience!

Summary:

Visual Content is just going to get bigger and bigger and it is imperative for marketers to integrate this into their content marketing strategy. We read how Matt recommended some easy to implement tactics for Pinterest marketing. To many it may sound like one more social media platform to manage but if your target audience is skewed more towards female users and you are an e-commerce company then you just cannot afford to not have an active presence on Pinterest. Again, social media is all about execution so go ahead and start implementing all the tips as recommended by Matt Siltala. And as it goes "Happy Pinning"

CHAPTER 7

CONTENT MARKETING FOR B2B LEAD GENERATION

WITH ARDATH ALBEE

Introduction:

There is one question that I get asked by our cohorts at Instant E-Training all the time and that is B2B Social Media is different than B2C Social Media. It is not as the underlying strategies are the same whether it is B2C or B2B. The same way most businesses think B2B content marketing is a different beast altogether. The fact is yes you are focused on generating leads in B2B so the hooks you employ to capture leads might be slightly different but a lead for a B2B company is same as a sale for a B2C company. In this chapter, we have Ardath Albee who will be going in greater detail in all areas of B2B lead generation with content marketing. So without any further ado, here's Ardath....

Content Marketing For B2B Lead Generation:

56% of B2B buyers are dissatisfied with their buying experience:

People want to reach out when they are interested, they have no desire to be hounded by you until that point. Buyers are now pushing vendors back in their sales process. 51% do not want to interact with a solution provider until they have established a list of potential vendors.

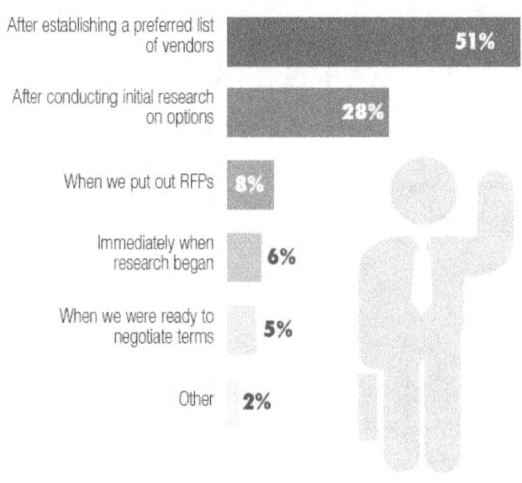

At what point did you interact with a contact from the solution provider?

DemandGen Report, 2012

Definition of a B2B lead: a person with priorities related to job responsibilities that your solutions and services address.

Buyers are looking for a company that closely resembles their best accounts and those whom are open for a conversation. 67% of buyers still don't trust vendor content and as such we need to strive to gain that trust. Let us consider how the buyer approaches gathering information and what motivates them to begin searching.

How do you initiate your information process?

Most people start with informal research around a business challenge. They will start by conducting anonymous inquiries of a select group of vendors via websites and other public information. They will then engage with peers who have addressed a similar challenge. This is where social channels come into play. We may not necessarily be able to sell to everyone, but we can put our content in front of many to help to seal our good reviews from peers and colleagues. Many prospects follow industry conversations of the topic they are concerned with and use that knowledge to engage with one or more potential service providers.

After your Initial search what was your next step?

Once people have gathered a starting point of information, they develop a short list of potential services or solutions to discuss internally. The initial information was collected to build the business case needed. Relevant internal stakeholders are then looped in and internal budgeting discussions are initiated.

B2B lead generation has changed:

In the past there was a quicker turnover of leads. Any form filled out was sent to sales and they called the prospect. Nowadays, lead generation takes longer and it is a nurturing process. When the lead is ready to explore what you can offer, they will think of you. This is all accomplished by creating content to supply your following.

How do I shift to the new school way?

Content is supposed to provide 3E's: education, expertise and evidence. Content must engage, inspire and motivate action! You have to stand out from all your competition by offering something they don't. You may be able to provide content that helps to solve a problem that no one else has foreseen. Think about the huge impression you will make then.

Earn trust:

Studies show that buyers see emails as important. If you send an email providing a new piece of information and the recipient clicks on the link, they are likely to pay more attention to your future emails. This is also a great way to humanize your brand by providing information that you found useful or relevant.

Match relevance to recipients:

Keep your subject line under 50 characters and focus on one point. Provide two calls to action, one can be a hyperlink on a key phrase and one directive such as 'read more.' Use a double tap method. One email will provide one perspective, the other will provide a completely different take based on the same original piece of content. Segmenting your audience in this manner will allow you to maximize one piece of content for two demographics. You do not want to handle your audience with an iron fist but rather gently bring them around to embracing your content. If you receive engagement, send an email that suggests a similar article to one that they have just opened and try to hold onto their engagement for longer.

Use personalization differently:

You do not want to come across as superficial or insincere. Personalization should not be obvious, so try to scale it back to a human level, your voice should simply blend into your messaging and your content. Use words and phrases that your customers would use and focus on the problems that they need to solve. Leave out your products and focus only on the solutions you can offer. Maintain a friendly conversational level. You should be thinking how you can provide them with a story that they can share and talk to them not at them. You want to come across as an ally that wants to help them. Only then you can be considered an expert.

Remember, a stranger is never an expert.

Lead scoring must be a priority:

Lead scoring allows us to measure what is happening so that we can identify and track how likely people are to become buyers. We have to engage with leads and without scoring we cannot discern patterns about who is the right person to engage with at the right time with the right content. We have to consider what the person reading our content is doing next. Are they reading more articles on the same topic? When the pattern that emerges from an original piece of content is identified, it can be decided how best to proceed and if sales should call them to inform about a solution you can offer. This will help you identify opportunities for momentum. Not only do we have to get their interest, we have to deliver value. Identify their status quo of what isn't working for them and how they can fix it with your help.

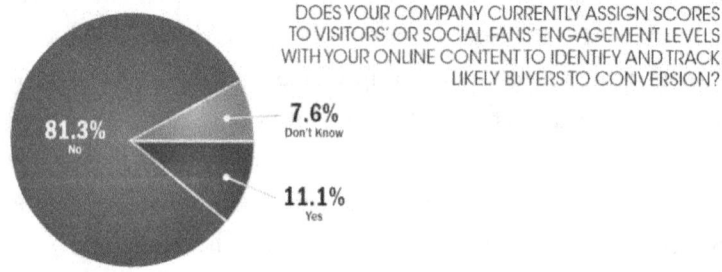

Lead Scoring Must Become a Priority

Lead Generation should be a natural outcome

When you create any piece of content say it be a video, a blog post, eBook or any other form of content then lead generation should be a natural outcome. Every piece of content should have some form of lead capturing mechanism so the flow of information is two ways.

Lead Generation Should be a Natural Outcome

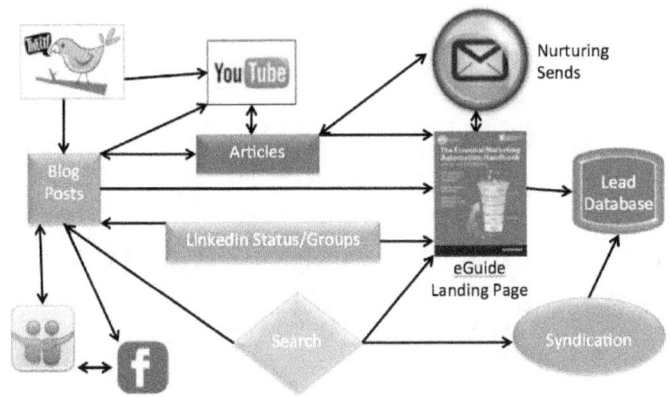

When prospects share your ideas:

When prospects share your ideas you are put into the room even when your sales team is not. Reportedly, 73% of buyers are looking for ideas they can share and discuss. On average, 5 IT decision makers need to consume 5 pieces of content before they are ready to be contacted by a sales rep. Understanding consumption patterns is critical for determining lead quality and sales transition, or ramping engagement to get there. Not informing yourself will cause you to shoot yourself in the foot. Keeping all these ideas in mind will surely help to ensure that you get yourself in the room!

Summary:
Lead generation is at the top of every B2B marketers list and content marketing can be a great way for marketers to generate those leads at a low Cost Per Lead (CPL).

CHAPTER 8

BUILDING A CONTENT MARKETING TEAM

WITH MICHAEL WEISS

Introduction:

Most companies live in a resource constraint world. We all are trying to do more with less and content marketing is no different. A common question I get from our cohorts at Instant E-Training is how should they go about the content creation process as they either have few or none in their content marketing team. A big part of content marketing is you guessed it – about creating content and that means you need to have a team and a process in place that can execute on your content marketing strategy. In this chapter, we have Michael Weiss, a longtime content marketing expert, to share some of his insights on how to go about building a content marketing team in your company or outsourcing it. Over to Michael now!

How do we decide to outsource?

Limitations cause us to outsource. We can have limited skills, time or resources so it makes sense to outsource when there is an internal limitation. No matter how fabulous we are, we don't always have a certain necessary skillset!

Tip: Look within and ask simple questions.

Start with the why:

Firstly, you must decide the audience you want to engage with. You will end up creating different stories to cater for the variety of your audience needs. You might have a million exciting ideas, but who is going to do all this work? Start with *who:* knows how to write, make videos, design etc. You will start to establish two critical things, what you have and what you need. By understanding what skills you have within your organization, you can see what skills you do not have in house. This will help you to establish a plan.

Don't become tactic happy!

Consistently creating content that has solid brand messaging and standards, is unrealistic. You will have to remain focused to be able to show results. Reportedly, we are hit with over 3,000 advertising messages per day. Mastering content marketing is imperative so that we can rise above the clutter and noise. Let's consider the roles and responsibilities that can help effectively implement a content marketing strategy and whether they can be sourced internally or externally.

Content Marketing Team Org Chart

Chief content officer: (CCO) owns the content strategy, is accountable for its success. Generally, only the largest companies have the luxury of appointing someone this role.

Chief listening officer: Vital for success. The CLO monitors customer activities and analyzes the analytics, this person could be a community manager and may be outsourced. It is report based and therefore the person in charge does not need to have an in-depth understanding of your business model but will need a basic grasp.

Managing editors: Own the channels. They are the people that have the final say in what content that is run. Reports to the CCO (if possible) and manages what is happening in their channels. Chances are they own more than one channel and if at all avoidable, shouldn't be outsourced.

Content producers: Manage the content creation process, they do not necessarily create the content but manage the resources. They are highly detailed, able to motivate and can handle stress. This can be outsourced, the person is in charge of resources, scope scheduling and budget.

Content creators: This is almost always outsourced as it is rare that you will have designers, videographers, writers and general content creators on your internal team.

Subject Matter Experts: Key to your success. These are not necessarily writers, but the people that hold the knowledge of what you do. These people are great resources to your writers as they can pull the required information out of them to create your content. They are never outsourced! Customer service is a gold mine in this respect as they are hearing on a daily basis what is working, what is not, what the problems are and what solutions you can provide.

Once you have identified your internal resources and what you require to be filled externally, you must establish your content creation flow. It should start with the CLO as they are the people with their fingers on the pulse of what is engaging and what is not. They know that your social media isn't engaging, your infographics are doing fine but your videos are thriving! They need to bring their insights to the managing editors. The managing editors take on board the valuable information the CLO has provided and call a meeting with the content creators. The content creators are informed of the Chief Listening Officer's findings and the analytics they provided to back up their claims. With this guidance, they are given a deadline and must collaborate with the writers. Writer one, should work for the company, writer two can be outsourced. The designers, videographers and writers then need to reach out to the SMEs. Remember, one person can take on more than one role. Depending on the size of your organization you can adorn someone with more than one hat.

Content can come from something as simple as the CLO noticing that there are recurring posts appearing around the one product issue. Writer one, needs a SME to interview so they can obtain all the answers that they need to help them write their piece. If it is product related, they need to speak to someone within the organization that helped to create the product that the consumer is having issues with. Once they have received that and composed their piece; designers, videographers and any other necessary skillsets are brought into the fold to help make the piece aesthetically pleasing. The content is then brought back to the managing editor for approval and feedback. They sign off and your team has successfully created a piece of contact.

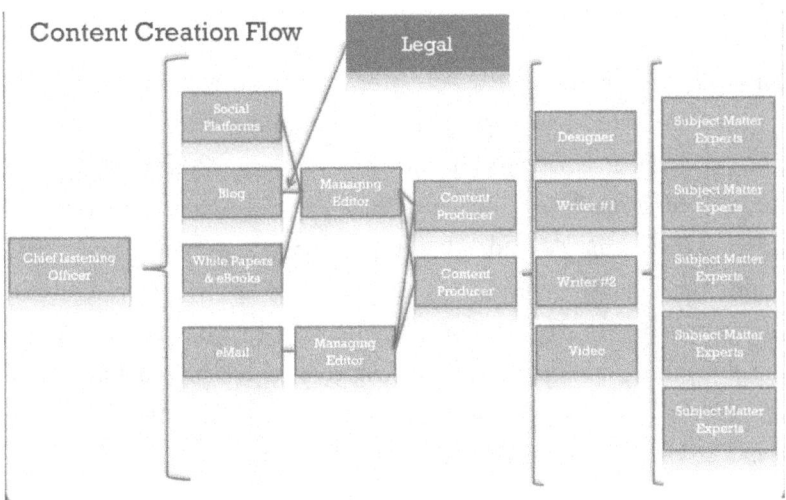

A sample of Content Marketing Flow

You will need legal to review any content before it is posted. You do not necessarily need to go to a lawyer, there is someone in your organization that is fully aware of policy that can sign off to ensure that what you are posting is not stepping on anyone's toes. This will help ensure that you do not publish on a platform that you shouldn't have or break any company posting guidelines and ultimately stay out of hot water!

When you have gained some traction with your content, you can reconsider your needs and whether or not you need to outsource more work. You should not outsource more than you are comfortable with, but you will need to consider supply and demand!

Summary:

I am hoping after reading this chapter you have a better idea into how you could structure your content marketing team. It doesn't matter if you are a two person startup or a large 20,000 employee company. Everyone faces the same resource constraint realities in business. That being said, having a process and role and responsibilities clearly defined you will see how your content marketing process is streamlined. After all, your goal should be to become a content creation machine where you are producing useful and relevant content for your target customers. As Michael wrote earlier in the chapter "Don't become tactic happy!"

CHAPTER 9

DATA DRIVEN CONTENT MARKETING

WITH KAILA STRONG

Introduction:

Throughout this book we learned about different content marketing tactics that businesses can implement. In this chapter, we look at a different method of content marketing and that is through data. Data helps us become informed marketers and as a result we can take existing data from various sources like site analytics, customer calls, and other sources to create or refine our content marketing tactics. In this chapter, Kaila Strong of Vertical Measures will list some of the data driven tactics she utilizes to create amazing content. Over to Kaila now....

Data driven Content Marketing:

What is it? "Utilization of data, statistics, market research, surveys, and/or public data to dictate a content strategy."

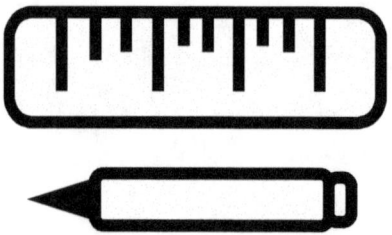

What's important to measure?

It is possible to become a bit inundated with the huge amount of data that can be measured. Decide what is relevant to you, generally the most important areas are: demographics, traffic, social metrics, links, email metrics. Who is looking at your content, where is the traffic coming from and what are they doing when they arrive?

Demographic Data:

This provides important insights into trends and opportunities that may exist in a market. Use this information to develop content catered to your audience. Determines market segments and do some research to establish who your customer really is. Use social information if you have it or create a survey. Be aware of their age, income, education, location etc. Using this information will help you create content that caters directly to your prospects.

Target Marketing:

Be focused with your message, for example, getting Geo-specific could help you include real world issues in your content. Social demographics will provide you with a vision of what your customer looks like. Look for the people that are in your niche. Review competitors to see what they are doing as part of their content marketing efforts and then create your buyer personas. This will require you sitting down with your team and determining who your audience is. This will help you to create and implement ideas around a particular area of focus.

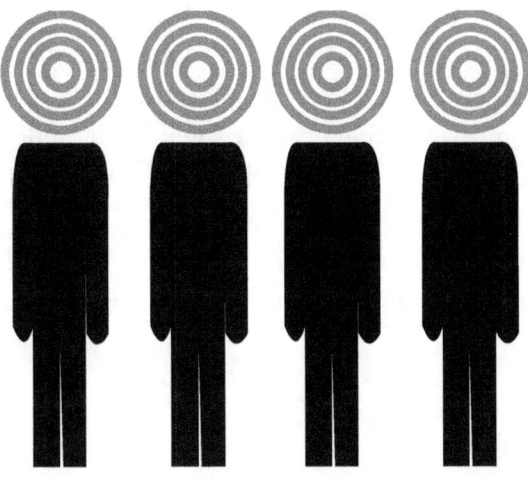

Traffic Data:

Review the most viewed pages to discover the popular content on your site and then use that data to develop new content. Content will attract people, but other content will help with conversions and keep them engaging with your site for longer. Look at quarterly, yearly and beyond to determine your trends. Examine the day and time on the page and look for cyclicality and peaks. Some posts do extremely well over the course of a year but do not necessarily do well over a month. That is why examining data sets will help to give you a clear understanding of what is working. Look at your referral sources when analyzing too so that you can see where people are driven to your content from.

Tip: Analyzing the time spent on your page will help you to create the right length of content for your followers will not necessarily read your entire piece but you want to ensure they get the key takeaways.

Social Metrics:

Insight into the most socially active content can be a key data set to examine. Look for content that your social audience appreciates and feels compelled to share, like, tweet and comment on.

Determine the most social type of content and understand who engages with your content. This will help you identify the best platforms to utilize for content distribution. Examine your most popular content each month, quarter and year. This will help you to create consistently engaging content. It may not be worth your while

to look in-depth on a monthly basis but you should keep an account even if it does not delve in extremely deeply. Tracking your referral will allow you to create content catered to a popular platform. For example if a lot of your referral traffic is coming from Twitter, you will need to factor in the 140 maximum characters in your strategy, whereas if you notice a huge flow from Pinterest, you should consider creating more visual content.

Link Data:

"Discover your top pages in Open Site Explorer, the pages that are linked to the most. Look to develop content that earns links."

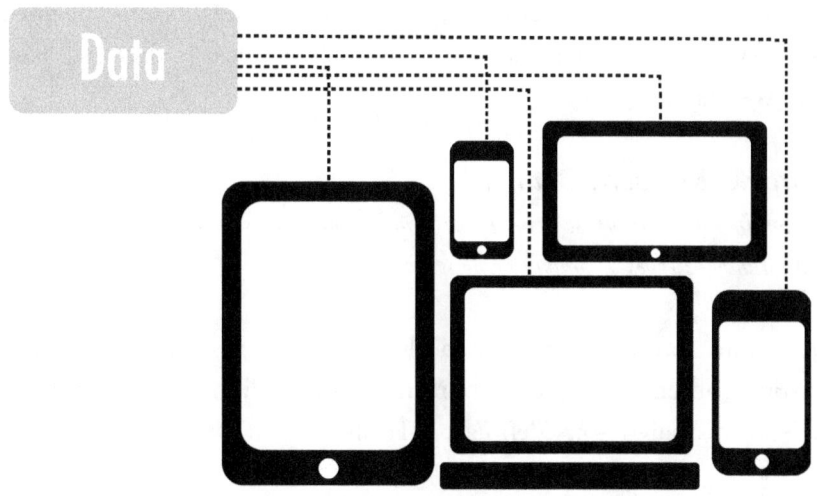

Discover your link bait content then examine your anchor text and authority of links.

Be relevant and become a resource worth linking to! If you are finding specific pieces and topics are doing well, try and replicate that success when you are creating new content.

Remember: Longer posts get more results than shorter and videos are very well received.

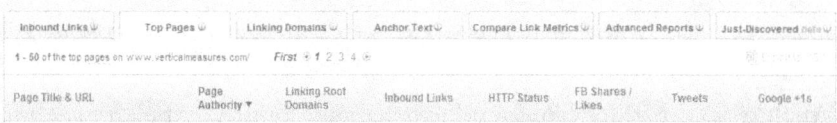

E-mail Metrics:

"Examine open rates, click through rates and data from e-mail campaigns, newsletters and the like."

Find patterns in high performing e-mail campaigns. Scrub your email lists if you are receiving a lot of non-deliverables as this will skew your results.

Search & Keyword Data.

"Examine data from search engine traffic, internal search and keywords to understand the types of content being searched for."

Delve into your site to search and look at keywords sending traffic to existing content. Uncover opportunities for additional content. Look in Google Analytics & Webmaster Tools.

Conversion Data.

"Conversion data can help you figure out which content pieces aid in converting traffic into sales. The highest converting type of content should be replicated to improve profits over time."

Define what a conversion is for you and then set up proper conversion tracking. This concerns more than the number of leads data. Rather, what actually closed? Tracking this will help you to determine what content is worth replicating for ROI.

Engagement Data.

Simply put, this is how your audience interacts with your content both on-page and off-page. You must understand methods of engagement.

Analyze where your demographic is hanging out. Are they retweeting you on Twitter or are they commenting on your Facebook statuses? Examine which of your call to actions are receiving engagement and where your content is been reposted. The platform where your content is receiving the most engagement is where you should be focusing your main efforts. In page analytics can help you.

Third Party Data.

Third parties discover data and share publically in case studies or reports, which can aid in understanding large groups.

Marketing surveys are a great way to collect impartial third party feedback. You can also set up Google alerts for industry data reports so that you stay abreast of any newly discovered findings within your industry.

Data driven content marketing best practices:

Test any data you acquire to ensure it's accurate. You should be striving to create a data driven organization.

Do not make assumptions about your data.. It is important to review your data regularly, so allocate someone the responsibility of analyzing your data over a predetermined period whether it be it weekly or monthly. This will help you track what is working in your campaign and what is not, which in turn will help you with your future content creation efforts.

Drive innovation with your data and share data with other departments as they could also utilize it. Focus on quality over quantity, you do not need pages of data irrelevant to your needs. There is no point in continuing to send updates to members of your list who are not opening them as it is unlikely you will see any ROI from these people. Introduce metric driven goals into this aspect of your campaign to help keep you on track.

Remember: Successful content strategies examine data driven content marketing principles.

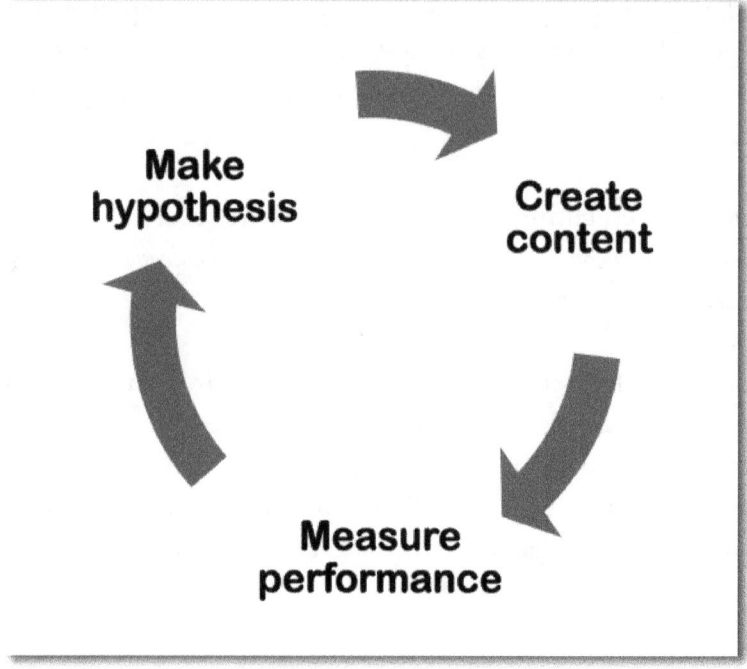

CHAPTER 10

FIVE KEYS TO SUCCESSFUL CONTENT MARKETING

WITH HEIDI COHEN

Introduction:

Content marketing is something that we frequently hear referenced daily in articles, blogs and campaigns. But when we take a second to actually consider the amount of content we consume on a daily basis, it becomes abundantly apparent just how important the content we create and curate actually is. This chapter is dedicated to the five keys to successful content marketing.

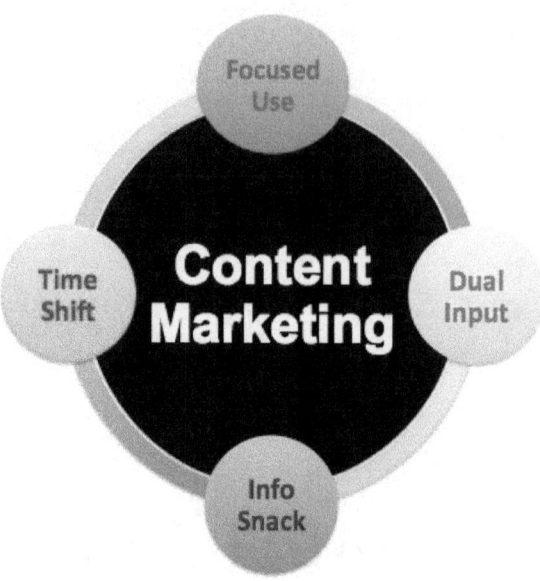

KEY 1: Create enduring corporate assets:

Align your content marketing objectives with business goals. You do not want to have your content marketing efforts in a separate area. These goals should be both specific and measurable; for example you might be trying to build your brand, drive traffic or generate leads. This will help establish your brand, attract customers and ultimately increase profits. Incorporate your brand into every piece of content to make yourself identifiable. This isn't necessarily just a logo, font and colors will also play a role. Build your own media entities which are corporate assets. When establishing your approach, you should think 'could I survive without Google?' Media assets such as an email list, website and blog are all additional resources that will help you prevail in the face of budgetary restrictions for example.

Tip: Your blog should provide value and not just focus on you. – Include light bulb where there is a asterisk

KEY 2: Meet customers' information needs:

Show rooming: people find out about your product and may check it out in person, but will ultimately end up online to research it. Create

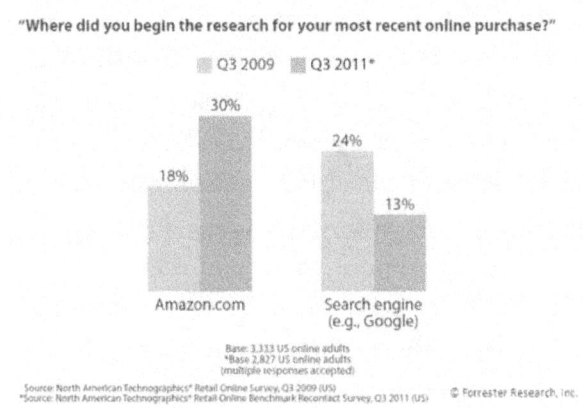

Amazon's Influence on Consumers Is Greater Than Google's

your marketing persona, think: who, what, which, where? Who is your target, what's the content and context, which channels/platforms and finally where is it shared? Provide useful content at every step of the purchase. The moment of truth comes when the prospect recognizes their need and goes online to research a potential product. If your competitor has better information on the product/service than you, who do you think will get the commitment from the consumer? When creating your content, you should be answering your customers' questions. If you are in the food industry for example, consider creating useful videos by sharing step-by-step recipes. You have the opportunity to link back to your products, but are fulfilling a customers' need by providing them with a useful resource. Provide multiple entryways to your content. Having only one track limits your customers' access and in turn means you are not meeting your customer needs. You are providing an answer, so you want to be sure that people are aware of that.

KEY 3: Stand out in a sea of content:

You may have the greatest content, but if no one is seeing it, it's a waste. You will need to create an editorial content calendar filled with value. Days are an important factor to consider during creation, your work week doesn't necessarily correspond with when your content is being used. Working on a monthly basis can seem daunting, but there are a few tricks! *Evergreen content* are your major pieces, consider them as your pillar content and a valuable reference. This content addresses a question that people are always asking and as such never goes out of demand. *Just in time content* is the opposite. This content is essentially taking advantage of trending topics. A few examples are holidays, local events, or personalities. You don't want to be out of sync with your public and general trends. You can reuse content so things stay contextually relevant by offering value once again. *Curate content*, but be careful! You do not want to infringe on other peoples' copyright but you want to add value to other people's content by adding your own perspective. There is an argument for using as much of your own content as others. Be sure to give credit and air on the side of caution. *Co-create content* by involving your customers and encourage sharing. Most people appreciate recognition so they should be happy to oblige.

KEY 4: Integrate content with other marketing & communications:

Audit your content by compiling an inventory of your existing content, catalog, assess, and determine where your content gaps exist. When you have done this, you can decide what content you should create or reuse. Structure your content by identifying what topics have been covered, what keywords you have used, and the format of your content, (aka how easy it is to consume). You will want to approach this by keeping your consumer and influencers in mind. How you can make your product stand out and how can you get people thinking about it? Next, you will want to think about how you can distribute your content, how you can align it with all your other marketing efforts, and how you can get the most out of it. For example, you can leverage your blog, share on social media, or put it in your newsletter. Remember that internal promotion in a company with loads of employees also has a huge extended reach.

Tip: Promoting your content can be tricky, but here are a few ideas: incorporate it into your advertising, cross promote on other content, ask influencers to share, or consider writing guest articles.

KEY 5: Budget for content marketing:

Most research shows that if budget is not the number one factor, it is a close second! Sourcing a budget for content marketing is extremely important. Determine what resources you need; are they editorial, writers, designers, or from a legal background? You want consistency and to be sure that you have access to this information. Planning will play a part in reducing cost as you can cover multiple bases with the one resource. When trying to source a budget you can explore both internal and external options.

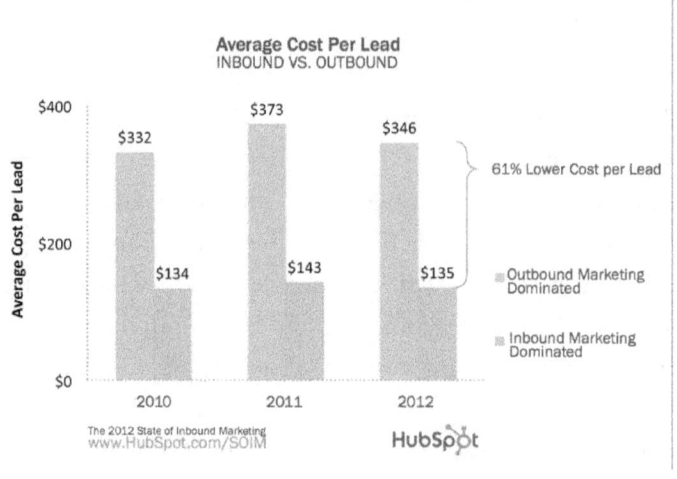

Internal	External
Website	Customers
PR	Government
Advertising	Social Media
Investor Relations	Events
Customer Service	Suppliers

Next, you will need to show how content marketing improves profitability. You want to show that you are giving information. Call to actions, targeted language pages, and a follow up process are all necessary components to help establish the success of your campaigns.

Tip: Remember different content exists throughout your organization.

CONCLUSION – FINAL THOUGHTS

Many of you may agree that throughout this book we learned new content marketing tactics from all our expert contributors. I would say if there is one common theme among all the chapters was the art of getting it done. Content marketing, and marketing in general, is about launching your campaign then collecting data and based on the data you go about optimizing it. Content marketing is no different and to me that is the underlying theme among all the chapters in this book that all our contributors presented. As Mark Zuckerberg famously said "Fail Fast, Fail Often"

Since this book was organized in a linear learning format where we started with content marketing strategy and build rest of the pieces on top of it along the way, it would help if I pick out some points from each chapter that resonated with me.

In Chapter 1 – we learned about the importance of establishing clear content marketing goals. Goals can be as basic like determining if you are trying to build brand, generate sales or leads from your content marketing. This makes a big difference as you need to have a desired outcome in mind before you start crafting your content marketing strategy.

In Chapter 2, we learned how to develop customer persona and the process you can follow to create a customer persona. Personas are very important and when done right can be of great help with your content marketing. The following is what you need to develop personas are Demographics, Behavior, Motivations, Challenges & Pain points, and customer concerns.

In Chapter 3, we learned how most searching behavior online can be grouped into three distinct categories of Inspire me, Educate me and Answer me. This in itself should be a critical component of your keyword research and content creation strategy if you simply follow the three distinct behaviors of online searchers.

In Chapter 4 we went into the nuts and bolts of SEO with a particular focus on on-page optimization. Among other things discussed in the chapter we learned that content optimization is about using the right keywords, having contextual relevance, engagement objects and about page level optimization. SEO is basic in nature but something that needs to be sustained over a period of time in order to perform better on search engines.

Chapter 5 was all about Social Media and how to leverage social media and Facebook in particular to drive content distribution. The one point from Brian Carter that resonated with me was the Facebook posting rule where 50% of the content you post can be curated, 30% of content could be original and 20% of content you post can be promotional in nature.

Chapter 6 was all about Visual Content Marketing and we learned from Matt Siltala on some of the approach we can take to succeed on Pinterest. An eye opener for me was the stat that 90% of information submitted to the brain is visual and images process 60,000 times faster than text, which is why Pinterest is thriving.

In Chapter 7 we learned the importance of content marketing for B2B lead generation. The point that resonated well with me was the importance of creating content with lead generation outcome in mind. Many times, businesses forget the natural outcome of creating content and that is to generate leads and Ardath Albee's chapter was a great reminder.

In Chapter 8 with Michael Weiss, we learned how if you should decide to create your content in-house or you should outsource it. Either way you would need to consider the roles and responsibilities that can help effectively implement a content marketing strategy and whether they can be sourced internally or externally. One of my key takeaways was not to become tactic happy!

In Chapter 9, Kaila Strong talked about how businesses can look at the most relevant data and come up with new content ideas. There are many different metrics businesses can look at but the most important question that you can answer with data is who is looking at your content, where is the traffic coming from and what are they doing when they arrive? That essentially is data driven content marketing.

Our final chapter was about the top 5 keys to content marketing with Heidi Cohen and it served as such a great reminder of all the things businesses need to consider to create awesome content for their customers!

I compiled this book and handpicked the chapters that made the most sense for businesses when starting out with content marketing. It was kept pocket sized to make it easily digestible and in the hopes that all the golden nuggets of information can be implemented by our readers.
Hope you had as much fun reading it that I had while writing it. And just like how I like to say to all our Instant E-Training members I would say this to you "Your results are commensurate with the efforts you put in digital marketing."

Happy Learning!

Continue Your Learning with Instant E-Training

All expert contributors for this book are trainers for Instant E-Training, an online digital marketing learning destination. Instant E-Training has hundreds of training videos and certification training in all areas of digital marketing including Content Marketing, Social Media, SEO, PPC, Web Analytics, Email Marketing and more. Our training videos are custom created by leading industry experts and at last count has videos from 100+ experts. With flexible on-demand plans, custom certification training with mentoring support, our members enjoy the best of on-demand and personalized digital marketing learning.

http://www.instantetraining.com/pricing-plans

All readers are eligible for an exclusive 10% off all our training plans. During checkout, Use **Coupon Code: BOOK10**

Praise for Instant E-Training

Cindy Yerkie, Hewlett-Packard (HP)

This is a must take comprehensive workshop on SEO. The workshop offers a good overview on all aspects of online marketing to help your SEO efforts. You will come away with great nuggets to improve your search efforts.

Rick Barron, Motorola

I recently completed the online Instant E-Training SEO Training Workshop. At first I was apprehensive in signing up for the course as I wasn't sure if this would be a workshop that would only provided half-baked information. Was I pleasantly wrong. Bob Tripathi and his guest speakers provided such a wealth of SEO information that I was overwhelmed.

Benin Brown, Rock-Bottom T-Shirts

Heavy on insight and light on fluff. This is exactly what you need in an online certification program dealing with Facebook, SEO, or social media in general. I highly recommend Instant E-Training to anyone wishing to move forward in any of these areas.

Lewis Hutcheons, Bar Code Integrators

I gained a lot of value from Instant E Training's SEO on-line Work shop. I gained a lot of information on site architecture, on-site SEO, link building, and analytical tools, and each speaker took a lot of time to answer questions at the end of the lesson as well as on the Q&A section of the site.

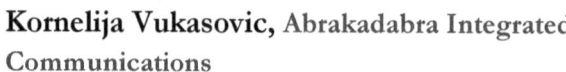

Kornelija Vukasovic, Abrakadabra Integrated Communications

Instant E-Training Social Media Certification program was a great experience. Team based project worked great due to my wonderful team members. I have learned many new things and it helped me improve social media strategy planning in my company. It is an experience that I would always recommend to people interesting in social media.

Digital Marketing Services with Instant E-Solutions

Instant E-Solutions was created to fulfill the digital marketing needs of scaling technology companies. The services offered by Instant E-Solutions range from consulting to fully fledged, hands-on digital marketing execution.

It is an boutique digital marketing agency that closely works with scaling tech companies in Chicago and elsewhere so that companies can focus on their core expertise of building great companies while we focus on supporting their growth objectives with our deep digital marketing domain expertise. Visit us at http://www.instantesolutions.com

Instant E-Solutions provides big agency results at start-up cost in the following areas.

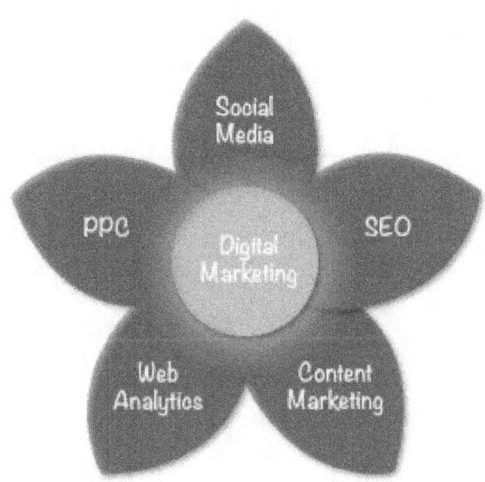

OUR CONTRIBUTORS

Heidi Cohen, President of Riverside Marketing Strategies @heidicohen

Heidi Cohen is the President of Riverside Marketing Strategies, an interactive marketing consultancy. She has over 20 years' experience helping clients increase profitability by developing innovative marketing programs to acquire and retain customers based on solid analytics. Clients include New York Times Digital, AccuWeather.com, CheapTickets, and the UJA. Prior to starting Riverside Marketing Strategies, Heidi held a number of senior-level marketing positions at The Economist, the Bookspan/Doubleday Direct division of Bertelsmann, and Citibank.

Arnie Kuenn, President of Vertical Measures @ArnieK

Arnie Kuenn is the president of Vertical Measures and author of Accelerate! Moving Your Business Forward Through the Convergence of Search, Social & Content Marketing. Vertical Measures specializes in providing strategic search, social and content marketing services, designed to help businesses grow by obtaining more traffic and conversions. Arnie is a frequent speaker at conferences such as PubCon, SMX Advanced, American Marketing Association, Online Marketing Summit, Social Media AZ, and the ASU Cronkite School of Journalism.

Shade Wilson, Founder & CEO, Scalability Project @ShadeWilson

Shade Wilson is the Founder and CEO of the Scalability Project and has over 15 years experience in marketing having worked at advertising agencies like DIMAC Direct and the Martin Agency, and internet start-ups like PrecisionIR and Snagajob. Shade is on the board of the Richmond Chapter of the American Marketing Association, an instructor for the Greater Richmond Small Business Development Center, and leader of Richmond Inbound, a HubSpot user group.

Michael Weiss, Managing Director of figure 18 @mikepweiss

As Managing Director of figure18, Michael is a dynamic force in the content marketing world as a veteran speaker and consultant. As a TED Talker and accomplished musician, Michael is no stranger to the stage and enjoys entertaining people whether they want to learn, rock out or both! He is the author of Pitch Elevation: Your Guide To Becoming A Better Presenter.

Ardath Albee, CEO of her firm Marketing Interactions, Inc., @ardath421

Ardath Albee, CEO of her firm Marketing Interactions, Inc., applies 25+ years of business management and marketing experience to help B2B companies with complex sales create eMarketing strategies that use contagious content platforms to turn prospects into buyers. Her book, eMarketing Strategies for the Complex Sale was published by McGraw-Hill. Ardath was recently selected as one of the 50 Most Influential People in Sales and Marketing for 2012 by Top Sales World and the Sales and Lead Management Association.

Brian Carter, Author & Speaker
@briancarter

Brian Carter, internationally bestselling author of three books: *The Like Economy, LinkedIn for Business* and *Facebook Marketing,* is one of the best known names in digital marketing and social media and is respected as an international authority on how organizations can generate bigger business results. His 18 years of business success guide The Carter Group, which strives to provide the best possible service and results in the digital marketing industry.

Kaila Strong, Vertical Measures @cliquekaila

Kaila Strong is an Account Manager with Vertical Measures, a Phoenix-based Internet Marketing company, where she manages client Internet marketing campaigns. Kaila also writes on the Vertical Measure's blog and is a frequent industry guest blogger.

Matt Siltala, President of Avalaunch Media @MattSiltala

Matt Siltala President of Avalaunch Media specializing in Content Marketing, Visualizing Data, Social Promotion, SEO & PPC.

ABOUT THE AUTHOR

Bob Tripathi has 12+ years of in-the-trenches experience in all areas of digital marketing having started with PPC and SEO in 2001. With a degree in international business and marketing, Bob taught himself to code and started his first company at 22. Since then Bob has worked with businesses across both B2C and B2B industries helping scale businesses with his digital marketing expertise. Bob also had stints with companies like Sears, Discover Financial Services and few others in specialized in-house internet marketing acquisition roles. His true passion for education and digital marketing led to Instant E-Training that he co-founded in 2011 and Instant E-Solutions shortly after. Bob is a frequent speaker at leading industry conferences like SES, SMX, Ad-Tech and many other conferences. Bob is also the founder of SEMPO Chicago Chapter and The Digital Marketing Group (DMG) Chicago.

ACKNOWLEDGMENTS

Instant Content Marketing Success would not have been possible without the assistance, contributions, and support of a great many wonderful people over the years.

First and foremost, I'd like to thank all of my wonderful trainers at Instant E-Training without whom this book would not have been possible. Special thanks to Arnie Kuenn of Vertical Measures for proposing the idea of a content marketing training program. Many thanks to all our contributors in this book including Heidi Cohen, Shade Wilson, Brian Carter, Matt Siltala, Michael Weiss, Ardath Albee, and Kaila Strong.

Second, I'd like to thank my staff for making this book possible starting with Rebecca McCarthy who helped convert lot of materials from video into text format. What started as a small eBook project turned out into a longer version eBook and then into its current form of a pocket sized book. I'd also like to thank our designer for many of the illustrations in the book, Chester Huang. I'd also like to thank our little tech community at Catapult Chicago for the "we are in it together" feeling. You guys rock!

I'd also like to thank all my Instant E-Training trainers who have supported me all these years by either speaking at our training or mentoring me. Special thanks to Eric Enge for all your support, Brian Carter, Sima Dahl, Krista Neher, Lisa Buyer (your book was an inspiration), Bill Hunt, Chris Boggs, Alan K'necht, Hollis Thomases, Samantha Iodice, Brianna Carlton Rush, Christine Churchill, Shari Thurow, Stephan Spencer, Dan Zarrella, Neal Schaffer, Ashish Rangnekar, Angie Schottmuller, Jonathan Allen, Jessica Bowman, Bryson Meunier, Stoney deGeyter, Joseph Kerschbaum, Bernie Borges, Thom Craver, Elizabeth Brady, Marshall Sponder and many others that have helped play a part in making Instant E-Training what it is today. I sincerely thank you all. Finally, I'd like to thank some wonderful people who gave me the professional opportunity to rise and shine including my past bosses at Discover Financial Services namely Margo Georgiadis, Sarah Alter, Michelle Carlin, Steve Furman, Mike Boush, and many other wonderful coworkers. And above all I'd like to thank my family for giving me the gift to dream big in life, Caty for everything you did for me and finally my little poji Isabella for the bright light you shine in my life.

RESOURCE LIST

Chapter One: 10 Steps to building a Content Marketing Strategy. Source: KPCB.com
- 10 Steps to building a Content Marketing Strategy. Source: © 2013 Heidi Cohen (http://HeidiCohen.com) – All rights reserved

Chapter Two: Identifying and Developing the Buyer Persona. Source: http://www.soovle.com/
- Identifying and Developing the Buyer Persona. Source: Shade Wilson
- Identifying and Developing the Buyer Persona. Source: Shade Wilson
- Identifying and Developing the Buyer Persona. Source: Shade Wilson

Chapter Three: Keyword Research for Content Inspiration Building Source: Optify, inc.
- Keyword Research for Content Inspiration Building Source: http://www.soovle.com/
- Keyword Research for Content Inspiration Building Source: Google.
- Keyword Research for Content Inspiration Building Source: Google.

Chapter Four: Content Marketing for SEO:sportsauthority.com

Chapter Five: Content Marketing for Social Media. Source: Brian Carter.

- Content Marketing for Social Media. Source: Brian Carter.
- Content Marketing for Social Media. Source: Brian Carter
- Content Marketing for Social Media. Source: Brian Carter.

Chapter Six: Visual Content. Source Matt Siltala.
- http://mashable.com/2013/10/15/pinterest-referral-traffic/

Chapter Seven: Content Marketing For B2B Lead Generation. Source: **DemandGen Report, 2012.**

Chapter Eight: Building a Content Marketing Team: Source: Michael Weiss.
- Building a Content Marketing Team: Source: Michael Weiss.

Chapter Nine: Data driven Content Marketing. Source: Disney.

Chapter Ten: Five Keys To Successful Content Marketing. Source: Disney.
- Five Keys To Successful Content Marketing. Source: Forrester Research Inc.
- Five Keys To Successful Content Marketing. Source: HubSpot.

www.ingramcontent.com/pod-product-compliance
Lightning Source LLC
Chambersburg PA
CBHW051334170526
45166CB00002B/811